THE RACIAL POLICIES OF AMERICAN INDUSTRY

REPORT NO. 15

THE NEGRO IN THE TRUCKING INDUSTRY

by

RICHARD D. LEONE

*Assistant Professor of Management
School of Business Administration
Temple University*

Published by

INDUSTRIAL RESEARCH UNIT, DEPARTMENT OF INDUSTRY
Wharton School of Finance and Commerce
University of Pennsylvania

Distributed by

University of Pennsylvania Press
Philadelphia, Pennsylvania 19104

Copyright © 1970 by the Trustees of the University of Pennsylvania
Library of Congress Catalog Card Number 70-127854
ISBN: 0-8122-9059-3
MANUFACTURED IN THE UNITED STATES OF AMERICA

FOREWORD

In September 1966, the Ford Foundation announced a major grant to the Industrial Research Unit of the Wharton School to fund studies of the Racial Policies of American Industry. The purpose of the research effort, now in its fourth year, is to determine why some industries are more hospitable to the employment of Negroes than are others, and why some companies within the same industry have vastly different racial employment policies, and to propose appropriate policy.

The studies have proceeded on an industry by industry basis, under the direction of the undersigned, with Dr. Richard L. Rowan, Associate Professor of Industry, as Associate Director. In addition, both Dr. Rowan and the undersigned have undertaken specific industry studies. This study of the trucking industry is the fifteenth in a series of reports dealing with specific industries. Already published studies include the automobile, aerospace, steel, hotel, petroleum, rubber tire, chemical, paper, banking, insurance, meat, tobacco, and coal industries. Soon to go to press are studies covering public utilities, railroads, lumber, urban transit, and shipbuilding. (See back cover for listings.) Other studies in progress will include various retail trades, air transportation, textiles, and several others. We are also completing books comparing and combining the findings of the various industry studies. The trucking study is scheduled for the book, *Negro Employment in Land and Air Transport,* which we expect to publish in 1971. Already published, or in press, are *Negro Employment in Basic Industry, Negro Employment in Finance, Negro Employment in Public Utilities,* and *Negro Employment in Southern Industry.*

This study is the work of Dr. Richard D. Leone, and is a revision of his doctoral dissertation in industrial relations, accepted by the Business and Applied Economics faculty of the University of Pennsylvania in May 1969. Dr. Leone wishes to thank Professor Rowan, chairman of his dissertation committee for guidance and assistance; Professor John S. de Cani, for advice on statistical techniques and sampling methodology; and representatives of government, industry, and the Teamsters' Union who gave so much of their time to assist. He also wishes to thank

Miss Mary McCutcheon, who typed both the dissertation and the book manuscript; Mrs. Rosamond J. Sanderson, who edited the manuscript; and Mrs. Margaret E. Doyle, who cared for numerous administrative problems. Besides assistance from the Ford Foundation grant, Dr. Leone's study also received support from the Labor Relations Council of the Wharton School. Errors or shortcomings are, of course, the sole responsibility of the author. In most previous reports, as in this one, the data cited as "in the possession of the author," have been carefully authenticated and are on file in our Industrial Research Unit library.

> HERBERT R. NORTHRUP, *Director*
> Industrial Research Unit
> Wharton School of Finance and Commerce
> University of Pennsylvania

Philadelphia
June 1970

TABLE OF CONTENTS

PAGE

FOREWORD iii

CHAPTER

I. INTRODUCTION 1

The Scope of the Study 2

Methodology 3

II. THE TRUCKING INDUSTRY 8

Governmental Regulation 9

Industrial Structure 10

For-Hire Carriers' Share of the Transportation
Market 11
Industrial Concentration 13
Industrial Location 16

Manpower 18

Occupational Distribution 19
Unionization 20
Future Employment Needs 22

III. NEGRO EMPLOYMENT PRIOR TO 1960 25

Social Influences 28

Teamster Influence 29

IV. NEGRO EMPLOYMENT IN THE 1960's 33

The Overall Picture 33

The 1967 Sample 35
The 1968 Field Sample 38

The Road Drivers 40

Driver Qualifications 40
Negro Availability 42
The "Loss of Customers" Argument 46
The Reaction of White Employees 47
Approaches to Recruitment 48

CHAPTER   PAGE

    Seniority Provisions 53
    Grievance Procedures 55
    The Availability of Public Accommodations 57
    Nearness to Negro Labor Markets 57

    Local Drivers and Helpers 58

    Nondriver Manual Workers 60

    Management Personnel 61

        Middle Management 62
        Dispatchers 63

    Clerical Workers 63

    The IBT and Civil Rights 64

  V. REGIONAL AND CITY DIFFERENCES, 1968 68

    Negro Employment in the Northeast 68

    Negro Employment in the South 74

    Negro Employment in the Midwest 82

    Negro Employment in the West 83

 VI. GOVERNMENT EQUAL OPPORTUNITY ACTION AND IN-
     DUSTRY RESPONSE 94

    Investigation and Response 95
    Impact in Industry 96

    The Post Office, the OFCC, and Affirmative Action 101

        Affirmative Action in Practice 105
        Later Developments and Progress 106
        Training as Affirmative Action 110
        Sanctions under the Executive Order 113

    Court Proceedings 114

        Richard Johnson, Jr., v. Georgia Highway Express .. 114
        Lee v. Observer Transportation 117
        Hairston v. McLean Trucking Company 118
        James v. Braswell Motor 119
        Bradshaw v. Associated Transport, Inc., and United
          States v. Associated Transport 120
        United States v. Roadway Express 122

CHAPTER PAGE

United States v. Central Motor Lines, Inc. and Locals 71, 391, and 710, International Brotherhood
of Teamsters _____ 123

Administrative Problems in Civil Rights Enforcement.. 124

The Role of the American Trucking Associations_____ 127

VII. CONCLUDING REMARKS _____ 130

APPENDIX

A. Sample Selection _____ 133

B. Expansion of the Employment Data and Determination of the Coefficient of Variation for Four Geographical Areas _____ 141

C. Post Office Department Guidelines on Affirmative Action under Executive Order 11246 _____ _____ 143

INDEX _____ 147

LIST OF TABLES

TABLE   PAGE

1 Trucking Industry, Number of For-Hire Carriers by Class, 1945-1967 _____ 12

2 Trucking Industry, Revenue Distribution among Regulated Freight Carriers, 1940-1967 _____ 14

3 The Eight Largest Public Carriers, 1968 _____ 15

4 For-Hire Carriers, Location of Headquarters in Selected SMSA's, 1966 _____ 17

5 For-Hire Carriers, Employment by Class, 1957-1966 _____ 18

6 Trucking Industry, Employment by Occupation, 395 Class I Motor Carriers, 1967 _____ 19

7 Trucking and Warehousing Industry, Employment by Race and Sex, United States and Regions, 1940-1960 _____ 26

8 Motor Freight Transportation and Warehousing (SIC 42), Employment by Race, Sex, and Occupational Group, United States, 1966 _____ 34

9 Motor Freight Transportation and Warehousing (SIC 42) Compared with All Industries and Manufacturing Industries, Employment by Race, Sex, and Occupational Group, United States, 1966 _____ 36

10 Motor Freight Industry, Employment by Race, Sex, and Occupational Group, 395 Class I Motor Carriers, 1967 _____ 37

11 Trucking Industry, Employment by Race, Occupation, and Company Size, United States, 1968 _____ 39

12 Tractor Trailer and Motor Vehicle Operators, Post Office Department Employment by Race, Selected SMSA's, 1968 _____ 44

13 Trucking Industry, Employers' Preferences as to Sources of Recruitment of Hourly Employees _____ 51

14 Trucking Industry, Employment by Race, Occupation, and Firm Size, Northeast Region, 1968 _____ 69

TABLE   PAGE

15 Trucking Industry, Employment by Race, Occupation,
    and Firm Size, Philadelphia SMSA, 1968 _____ 70

16 Trucking Industry, Employment by Race, Occupation,
    and Firm Size, New York SMSA, 1968 _____ 71

17 Trucking Industry, Employment by Race, Occupation,
    and Firm Size, Boston SMSA, 1968 _____ 72

18 Trucking Industry, Employment by Race, Occupation,
    and Firm Size, South Region, 1968 _____ 77

19 Trucking Industry, Employment by Race, Occupation,
    and Firm Size, Winston-Salem Greensboro SMSA,
    1968 _____ 78

20 Trucking Industry, Employment by Race, Occupation,
    and Firm Size, Birmingham SMSA, 1968 _____ 79

21 Trucking Industry, Employment by Race, Occupation,
    and Firm Size, Charlotte SMSA, 1968 _____ 80

22 Trucking Industry, Employment by Race, Occupation,
    and Firm Size, Atlanta SMSA, 1968 _____ 81

23 Trucking Industry, Employment by Race, Occupation,
    and Firm Size, Midwest Region, 1968 _____ 84

24 Trucking Industry, Employment by Race, Occupation,
    and Firm Size, Chicago SMSA, 1968 _____ 85

25 Trucking Industry, Employment by Race, Occupation,
    and Firm Size, St. Louis SMSA, 1968 _____ 86

26 Trucking Industry, Employment by Race, Occupation,
    and Firm Size, Detroit SMSA, 1968 _____ 87

27 Trucking Industry, Employment by Race, Occupation,
    and Firm Size, West Region, 1968 _____ 89

28 Trucking Industry, Employment by Race, Occupation,
    and Firm Size, Denver SMSA, 1968 _____ 90

29 Trucking Industry, Employment by Race, Occupation,
    and Firm Size, San Francisco SMSA, 1968 _____ 91

30 Trucking Industry, Employment by Race, Occupation,
    and Firm Size, Los Angeles SMSA, 1968 _____ 92

TABLE   PAGE

31 Trucking Industry, Total Employees and New Hires by
    Race, 19 Class I Carriers, January 1 to June 30,
    1968 _____ 108

32 Trucking Industry, New Hires by Race and Occupational
    Group, 358 Trucking Companies, January 1 to
    June 30, 1969 _____ 109

LIST OF FIGURES

FIGURE   PAGE

1 The Motor Carrier Industry _____ 4

2 Standard Industrial Classification _____ 6

CHAPTER I

Introduction

One hot summer day in 1967, a Negro youth noticed that there were relatively few black truck drivers on the streets of Cincinnati.

In the 90 degree temperature of Monday, June 12, as throughout the summer, Negro youngsters roamed the streets. . . . Negro youths watched white workers going to work at white-owned stores and businesses. One Negro began to count the number of delivery trucks being driven by Negroes. During the course of the afternoon, of the 52 trucks he counted, only one had a Negro driver. His sampling was remarkably accurate. According to a study conducted by the Equal Employment Opportunity Commission less than 2 percent of the truck drivers in the Cincinnati area are Negro.[1]

Unlike many other industries where factory walls can hide the number of Negroes employed, the trucking industry's racial composition, for the most part, is subject to public scrutiny. An awareness of the extremely low number of Negro truck drivers contributed to the Negro youths of Cincinnati interfering with deliveries made by white drivers. This event precipitated a racial confrontation. By the time the National Guard had left Cincinnati, there were sixty-three persons injured—twelve of them requiring hospitalization. If the number of lives lost and the amount of property destroyed are valid criteria to judge the seriousness of civil disorders, then this was a minor incident, but it easily could have escalated into a major one.

Like the young Cincinnati Negro, this study is concerned with the employment of blacks working in the for-hire segment [2] of the motor trucking industry. It is concerned not only with Cincinnati but with the nation as a whole, not only with the driver

---

1. *Report of the National Advisory Commission on Civil Disorders*, March 1968 (Washington: U.S. Government Printing Office), p. 26.

2. For-hire motor carriers are those providing transportation of freight that belongs to someone else, in contradistinction to private carriers who use their own vehicles or leased trucks under their direct control for moving their own goods in furtherance of a principal business activity other than transportation.

job category but also with other job classifications in the industry. It attempts to show why Negroes are employed in some jobs and by some firms and not in other jobs or by other firms. A major part of the study will be concerned with governmental efforts at promoting equal employment opportunities among public carriers, the effects of law in this field, and current industrial response to this governmental action.

The Teamsters' Union [3] exerts a powerful influence upon the trucking industry. We shall therefore examine the organizational structure of this union and the political and economic factors bearing upon it in order to examine at what level union decisions are made which influence the employment and promotion of Negroes. Likewise, union-management agreements will be studied to ascertain whether they inhibit Negro employment.

THE SCOPE OF THE STUDY

In 1968, there were an estimated 15,900,000 trucks [4] registered in the United States, exclusive of those owned by the government. All of these vehicles are owned and operated by what is referred to generically as the motor carrier industry, which consists of two broad subdivisions: "private carriers" and "for-hire carriers."

The private carriers, which are divided into farm and non-farm operators, comprise that heterogeneous group of firms which use their vehicles or leased trucks to move their own goods in furtherance of a principal business activity other than transportation. For example, although many oil refineries maintain large fleets of trucks, their primary business interest is not the sale of transportation services, but the sale of petroleum products. The following companies (none of which are included in this study) are in this category: Coca Cola, Sears Roebuck, Anheuser Busch, and American Telephone and Telegraph, owners of more trucks than any other private carrier.

For-hire or public carriers are those firms providing transportation for freight belonging to others. Depending on whether

---

3. The full title of the union is the International Brotherhood of Teamsters, Chauffeurs, Warehousemen and Helpers of America. This union subsequently will be referred to as the IBT or the Teamsters.

4. American Trucking Associations, *American Trucking Trends, 1968* (Washington: American Trucking Associations, 1969), p. 3.

they obtained their operating rights from a state regulatory agency or from the Interstate Commerce Commission, for-hire carriers are referred to respectively as intrastate or interstate operators. Interstate carriers are divided into common carriers and contract carriers.

Common carriers are those available to the general public to transport, at published rates, specific types of freight between points which the Interstate Commerce Commission, or a state or local authority, has authorized them to serve. Contract carriers operate under continuing contracts with one or a limited number of shippers. They assign vehicles to the customer, with or without drivers, to meet the specific trucking needs of individual shippers.

This study is limited to the racial employment practices of interstate common and contract carriers. Thus, the 3,397 Class I and Class II carriers,[5] regulated by the Interstate Commerce Commission as to rates and types of commodities transported constitute the industrial scope of this study. The entire industry is diagrammed in Figure 1.

The public interstate carriers have grown considerably since 1935, when they came under government regulation, and they comprise a relatively homogeneous unit in the field of transportation. In 1966 the 3,973 Class I and Class II carriers, including about 700 local cartage firms under the jurisdiction of the Interstate Commerce Commission, employed approximately 573,400 people.[6]

METHODOLOGY

Much of the information and data for this study were obtained through personal interviews, conducted throughout the country with representatives of the trucking industry, govern-

---

5. Regulated carriers with gross annual revenues averaging more than one million dollars over a three-year period are designated as Class I carriers and those with gross revenues averaging between $300,000 and one million dollars are considered Class II carriers. Class III carriers are those with annual revenues below $300,000. Data used in this study were obtained from *Trinc's Blue Book of the Trucking Industry* (1966 edition), published annually by Trinc Associations, Ltd., Washington, D.C.

6. American Trucking Associations, *op. cit.*, p. 23.

FIGURE I

The Motor Carrier Industry

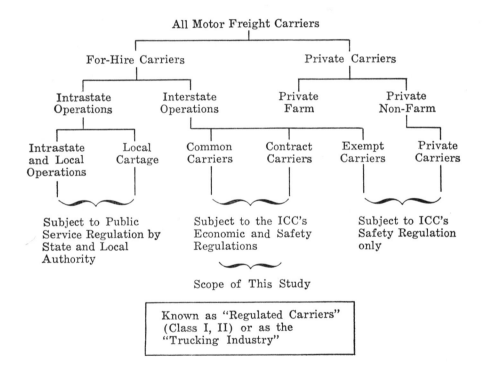

All Motor Freight Carriers

For-Hire Carriers — Private Carriers

Intrastate Operations — Interstate Operations — Private Farm — Private Non-Farm

Intrastate and Local Operations — Local Cartage — Common Carriers — Contract Carriers — Exempt Carriers — Private Carriers

Subject to Public Service Regulation by State and Local Authority

Subject to the ICC's Economic and Safety Regulations

Subject to ICC's Safety Regulation only

Scope of This Study

Known as "Regulated Carriers" (Class I, II) or as the "Trucking Industry" ment, and the union. This methodology necessitated establishing a representative sample of the carriers covered by this study. When officials of the selected companies were contacted, a pre-formulated questionnaire was used.[7]

Nonstructured interviews were used to obtain additional information from officials of the Teamsters' Union, from members of human relations and fair employment practice commissions, and from those in charge of public and private truckdriver training programs. Necessary background data were gleaned from publications of the U.S. Bureau of the Census, the Equal Employment Opportunity Commission, and other government and private sources.

Obtaining information about employment in the trucking industry presented a number of serious problems. For one thing, government data frequently lump together all types of trucking. In addition, the two-digit Standard Industrial Classification (SIC) No. 42, Motor Freight Transportation and Warehousing includes, as the name indicates, more than trucking. Since warehouse manpower policies involve less prestigious, and probably less skilled work, and a somewhat different employment environment, data included under SIC 42 must be evaluated carefully if they are to be at all meaningful for our purposes. In 1968, companies included under SIC 42 employed 1,056,100 people.[8] Figure 2 shows the trucking industry as delineated by SIC four-digit classifications. Our study covers a part of SIC 4213, for within this classification we find the 3,397 Class I and Class II interstate carriers which are of primary interest.

Moreover, information about the trucking industry's manpower is somewhat sketchy. As one comprehensive study noted, manpower data for the for-hire segment of the motor carrier industry "leaves us a great distance from the hard data which has

---

7. A copy of the questionnaire can be found in Richard D. Leone, O.S.F.S., "Negro Employment in the Trucking Industry: An Analysis of the Efforts of the Office of Federal Contract Compliance", unpublished Ph.D. dissertation, Philadelphia, University of Pennsylvania, 1969, Appendix III. See Appendix A for details of sample selection and Appendix B for statistical methods used.

8. *Employment and Earnings*, Vol. 15, No. 9 (March 1969). Table B-2, p. 61.

FIGURE 2

Standard Industrial Classification

SIC 42 MOTOR FREIGHT TRANSPORTATION AND WAREHOUSING

This major group includes establishments furnishing local or long distance trucking, transfer, and draying services, or engaged in the storage of farm products, furniture and other household goods, or commercial goods of any nature. The operation of terminal facilities for handling freight, with or without maintenance facilities, is also included. This group does not include delivery departments or warehouses operated by business concerns for their own use. Companies primarily engaged in the storage of natural gas are classified in SIC 4922.

SIC 421 TRUCKING, LOCAL AND LONG DISTANCE

SIC 4212 *Local Trucking and Draying, without Storage*

Companies primarily engaged in furnishing trucking, transfer, and draying services without storage, in a single municipality, contiguous municipalities, or a municipality and its suburban areas. Companies primarily engaged in collecting and transporting refuse by processing or destruction of materials are classified in SIC 4453.

SIC 4213 *Trucking, Except Local Companies*

Companies primarily engaged in furnishing "over-the-road" trucking service either as common carriers or under special and individual contracts or agreements.

SIC 4214 *Local Trucking and Storage, Including Household Goods*

Companies primarily engaged in furnishing trucking and storage services in a single municipality, contiguous municipalities, or a municipality and its suburban areas. Warehousing and storage of household goods when not combined with trucking is classified in SIC 4224.

Source: *Standard Industrial Classification* (Washington: U.S. Government Printing Office, 1967), p. 206.

proven so useful in other areas of transportation." [9] The discussion concerning the structure and growth of the industry, set forth in Chapter II, notes industry characteristics which make data collection difficult, and these characteristics also determine, to a considerable extent, the racial practices of the industry.

---

9. George Delehanty and D.K. Patton, *Manpower Profiles, Manpower Allocation and Labor Relations in Transportation, with Special Reference to the Trucking Industry* (Evanston, Ill.: Northwestern University Press, 1965), p. 42.

CHAPTER II

The Trucking Industry

Prior to World War I, trucks presented no real competitive threat to the railroads because (1) the trucks with their solid tires were equipped with low horsepower engines and thus could not travel at speeds in excess of fifteen to twenty miles an hour; (2) the trucks were so prone to breakdowns that distance, in the absence of garages and filling stations, was too great a risk; and (3) the century-old problem of adequate and dependable highways had not as yet been resolved. In spite of these shortcomings, however, the number of registered trucks increased dramatically from 2,200 in 1906 to 158,506 by 1915.

Because the war overburdened the railroads, the motor carrier industry was called upon to contribute to the transportation needs of a nation at war. This afforded the industry an opportunity to exhibit its value and usefulness as a swift, convenient, and economic medium in distributing goods. Truck registration increased from 158,506 in 1915 to 605,496 in 1918.[10]

In the 1920's and the early 1930's, trucking firms were usually small and family-owned, and nepotism in hiring prevailed. An enterprising risk-taker, after saving several hundred dollars or less for a down payment, procured a truck and found himself the president of a new trucking firm. Such firms, purchasing one truck at a time, were often financed by truck manufacturers who knew in advance that many of these men lacked the basic managerial skills needed to survive in a highly competitive market. Easy credit permitted almost unlimited entry into the industry and many searched in vain for fortunes acquired by relatively few. If successful, the owner augmented his fleet of trucks and, to keep costs down, hired his sons, cousins, in-laws, and friends, and, of course, few Negroes.

The small, family-owned and operated firms that were typical of the industry in its formative years were not likely to have Negroes in any but menial jobs. An exception must be made for the South, where driving had been considered a "Negro job" un-

---

10. American Trucking Associations, *American Trucking Trends, 1968* (Washington: American Trucking Associations, 1969), p. 3.

til the economic decline of the 1930's encouraged whites to accept such work. The southern carriers, however, often kept Negroes in an effort to keep the Teamsters' Union out. But once these firms were organized, wage rates and working conditions improved, and white employees sought employment with these companies. This is, of course, similar to the experience of Negroes in unionized construction in the South.

During the Great Depression, merchants neither had, nor could they borrow, the capital necessary to support large inventories. To minimize customer loss because of inadequate stocks, merchants turned more and more to the trucking industry, which met the needs of the times in two important respects: (1) trucks could transport small quantities of commodities swiftly; and (2) in the absence of federal regulations, trucks were willing to cut their rates in an effort to survive.

GOVERNMENTAL REGULATION

In the early 1930's, the federal government began to weigh the necessity of including trucking within the ambit of its transportation regulatory authority.[11] Federal intervention was prompted partially by pressure from the railroads, who were feeling the motor carrier industry's competitive presence, and also by the failure of the industry to practice uniform rules of road safety.

Against this background, Congress enacted the Motor Carrier Act (MCA) of 1935, which was amended as Part II of the Interstate Commerce Act of 1940, and amended several times since. Under the original and the amended Act, the Interstate Commerce Commission, assigned to administer the Act, does not regulate local cartage, that is, truckers who transport commodities within a radius of twenty miles. Also expressly excluded are all private carriers and haulers of agricultural commodities, but carriers hauling products manufactured from agricultural commodities are included.

The MCA provides regulation in the area of economics and safety requirements. The ICC has jurisdiction over the economic regulations, but its former authority to establish safety regulations, of which more will be said later, was transferred to the Department of Transportation in 1967. The economic regulations

---

11. William T. Ashby (ed.), *Motor Truck Redbook* (New York: Traffic Publishing Co., Inc., 1943), p. 94.

include: (1) the regulation of rates to stabilize rate competition through bureaus established for this purpose; (2) the mandatory certification of carriers in an effort to end unlimited and destructive entry; (3) the need for ICC approval of all consolidations if the number of vehicles exceed twenty; (4) the requirement that motor carriers file uniform reports with the ICC; and (5) the establishment of uniform insurance requirements.

In keeping with the underlying spirit of the Act, the ICC was supposed to restrict competition and this philosophy influenced interpretation of the law, especially the provisions concerning entry.[12] The MCA recognized that existing motor carriers had unilaterally staked out routes for themselves which the ICC could not radically alter. Consequently, the Commission had to grant certificates of public "convenience and necessity" to existing carriers under what came to be known as the "grandfather clause." The carriers had to prove that they had shipped substantial amounts of cargo, over specific routes, with a sufficient degree of regularity. The objective of discouraging entry by first recognizing existing routes was effective, and those wishing to start a trucking company had to demonstrate to the ICC's satisfaction that they were able and willing to perform the proposed service. As a result of the Motor Carrier Act, there began the trend toward a smaller number of larger carriers, which has continued to this day. This eliminated the smaller, possibly nonunion trucker who might have utilized Negro employees to a greater degree.

INDUSTRIAL STRUCTURE

The exact number of firms comprising the entire motor carrier industry is not known. Privately owned carriers are diffused throughout the entire economy and are difficult to identify. The ICC, nevertheless, estimates that there are between 55,000 and 60,000 private fleets throughout the country operated by a variety of shippers that are not transportation companies as such.[13] Unlike the private carriers, the for-hire carriers are com-

---

12. John B. Lansing, *Transportation and Economic Policy* (New York: The Free Press, 1966), p. 254.

13. Automobile Manufacturers Association, *Motor Truck Facts 1966*, pp. 42-43. Here can be found a list of the larger private carriers according to a broad industrial classification. Further editions of this publication do not contain a listing similar to the one noted above.

pelled to file comprehensive annual reports with the ICC.[14] As a result, from 1940 to the present, there has been made available a fairly consistent body of data relevant to the scope of this study.

The number of Class I, II, and III carriers has declined since 1945, but the industry as a whole has grown tremendously. The total ton-mileage has increased from 81,992,000 in 1946 to 388,500,000 in 1967, while the number of registered trucks has increased from 245,060 in 1945 to 690,097 in 1963.[15] Table 1 illustrates the carriers' decline in absolute terms, and indicates changes in criteria used to determine carrier classifications. For example, in 1945 a trucking firm was classified as a Class I carrier if its gross revenue was only $100,000 or more; since 1957 the break point has been raised to $1,000,000. Although the absolute number of Class II and Class III carriers has declined annually since 1951, except for 1959 and 1965, the number of Class I carriers has increased every year since 1940, except 1950 and 1967 when revenue requirements for the category were redefined upward.

For-Hire Carriers' Share of the Transportation Market

The trucking industry has grown primarily at the expense of the railroads. In 1940, for-hire motor carriers accounted for 10.0 percent of the total ton-miles shipped throughout the nation. Among other modes of transportation, the public carriers were third in the number of ton-miles hauled, because the railroads controlled 61.3 percent of this business and the waterways hauled 19 percent of all ton-miles moved in intercity transport. By 1966, the private carriers had doubled their share of all the transportation services rendered, accounting for 22 percent of the ton-miles hauled. From 1940 to 1967, the railroads' share declined from 61.3 percent to 43 percent, and the waterways' share fell from 19 percent to 15 percent.[16]

---

14. These reporting requirements are constantly revised. The *1966 Annual Report* for all Class I motor carriers was a comprehensive fifty-page document (Budget Bureau No. 60-R052.21). The *1966 Class II Annual Report* (Budget Bureau No. 60-R336.7), and the *Class III Annual Report* for the same year (Budget Bureau No. 60-R266.13) were forty-three pages and four pages, respectively. Class III carriers do not report their number of employees.

15. American Trucking Associations, *op. cit.*, p. 8.

16. *Ibid.*

TABLE 1. *Trucking Industry*
Number of For-Hire Carriers by Class
1945-1967

Year	Class I	Class IIa	Class IIIa	Total
	$100,000 or More	$25,000 to $100,000	Under $25,000	
1945	2,001	18,871		20,872
1946	2,099	19,019		21,118
1947	2,211	18,787		20,998
1948	2,507	18,337		20,884
1949	2,728	17,334		20,062
	$200,000 or More	$50,000 to $200,000	Under $50,000	
1950	2,053	17,544		19,597
1951	2,178	17,542		19,720
1952	2,361	17,001		19,362
1953	2,576	16,338		18,914
1954	2,640	15,694		18,334
1955	2,843	15,298		18,141
1956	2,939	14,957		17,896
	$1,000,000 or More	$200,000 to $1,000,000	Under $200,000	
1957	933	2,055	14,779	17,767
1958	988	2,167	14,105	17,260
1959	1,009	2,256	14,383	17,648
1960	1,053	2,276	12,947	16,276
1961	1,106	2,336	12,556	15,998
1962	1,148	2,495	12,340	15,983
1963	1,175	2,533	11,910	15,618
1964	1,195	2,536	11,748	15,479
1965	1,250	2,615	11,700	15,565
1966	1,298	2,675	11,453	15,426
1967	1,384	2,769	11,238	15,396

Source: *American Trucking Trends, 1968* (Washington: American Trucking
Associations, 1969), p. 13.

a Separate figures on Class II and Class III carriers are not available prior
to 1957. As of November 1968, Class II carriers must have revenues of
$300,000 to $1,000,000, while Class III carriers are those having revenues
below $300,000.

The awesome growth of the trucking industry and its relative share of the transportation market is demonstrated by an investigation of the revenue distribution among all the federally regulated carriers. Table 2 shows that in 1940 the trucking industry received 17.7 percent of the shippers' dollar. For the same year, the railroads received 75.4 percent of the dollars paid by the shippers. As shippers turned more and more to the motor carrier industry, the railroads' share of revenue dollars declined to 42.5 and the trucking industry increased its share to 49.3 percent. The loss of jobs by Negroes in railroad transportation was not, unfortunately, compensated for by an expansion of jobs in trucking.

Thus, despite the trend favoring bigger concerns, the trucking industry remains fragmented and, by comparison, one of small entrepreneurs. Highly competitive, the efforts of trucking companies have been narrowly directed toward immediate marketing and operating problems. The industry's personnel problems have not been given a high priority other than the need to get along with the Teamsters. Civil rights, as we shall note, falls in the somewhat neglected area of personnel.

By 1968, Class I, II, and III regulated public motor carriers accounted for 49.4 percent of the revenue received by all of the regulated freight carriers. In that year, however, only eight public motor carriers were found in the *Fortune* list of the top fifty transportation companies. In 1968, the Penn Central railroad ranked first among U.S. transportation companies, with slightly over two billion dollars in operating revenues. The largest trucking company, Consolidated Freightways, was nineteenth among all transportation companies, with operating revenues of $387,999,000. To further place trucking company size in perspective, it should be noted that ten railroads, seven airlines, and the Greyhound Corporation, among transportation concerns, had revenues in 1968 exceeding that of the largest trucking company, and that in terms of assets, the trucking companies are even more outdistanced by their air and rail competitors. Table 3 sets forth pertinent data for the eight trucking companies which are listed among the fifty largest transportation carriers.

Industrial Concentration

As the larger firms have grown, ease of entry has declined. General commodity haulers have decreased from 6,602 in 1957 to 5,566 in 1965. The increased dominance of larger firms be-

TABLE 2. *Trucking Industry*
Revenue Distribution among Regulated Freight Carriers
1940-1967

Year	Railroads Class I and II		Motor Carriers Class I, II, III		Water Carriers Class A, B, C and Maritime		Pipelines (oil)		Airways	
	Thousands of Dollars	Percent of Total	Thousands of Dollars	Percent of Total	Thousands of Dollars	Percent of Total	Thousands of Dollars	Percent of Total	Thousands of Dollars	Percent of Total
1940	3,686,375	75.4	867,000	17.7	85,394	1.7	225,760	4.6	22,719	0.5
1944	7,228,979	80.2	1,351,900	15.0	77,835	0.9	310,194	3.4	43,654	0.5
1948	8,271,158	71.1	2,698,100	23.2	190,396	1.6	377,034	3.2	89,765	0.8
1952	9,142,896	62.9	4,417,478	30.4	275,570	1.9	562,268	3.9	130,723	0.9
1956	9,320,230	56.8	5,828,877	35.5	335,351	2.0	737,386	4.5	180,508	1.1
1960	8,390,026	49.4	7,213,911	42.5	335,257	1.9	770,417	4.5	278,118	1.6
1963[a]	8,507,630	45.8	8,548,257	46.0	301,092	1.6	840,260	4.5	371,384	2.0
1965[a]	9,286,628	44.1	10,068,243	47.9	314,070	1.5	903,817	4.3	463,327	2.2
1966[b]	9,750,959	43.6	10,853,300	48.5	328,200	1.5	941,100	4.2	502,616	2.3
1967[b]	9,606,418	42.5	11,165,000	49.3	313,200	1.4	993,300	4.4	550,517	2.4

Source: *American Trucking Trends 1969* (Washington: American Trucking Associations), p. 9.

Note: Included are revenues of federally regulated carriers only; a major portion of the traffic handled by motor and water carriers is not subject to this regulation—for example, not reflected are the revenues or value of service generated by intrastate, local and exempt for-hire and private motor carriers. The total value of all motor carrier services would approximately triple the 10.9 billion shown in 1966; consequently, this table does not compare the economic significance of different modes of transportation.

[a] Revised figures for 1963 and 1965.

[b] Estimated figures for 1966 and 1967.

TABLE 3. *The Eight Largest Public Carriers, 1968*

Company and 1968 Rank among Transportation Companies	Headquarters	Operating Revenues	Assets	Net Income	Invested Capital	Number of Employees	Net Income as Percent of	
		Thousands of Dollars					Operating Revenue	Invested Capital
Consolidated Freightways	(19) San Francisco	387,999	192,851	13,963	70,993	16,523	3.6	19.7
Leaseway Transportation	(30) Cleveland	222,535	189,824	7,144	36,671	11,000	3.2	19.5
Roadway Express	(35) Akron	183,832	81,725	7,505	45,245	10,448	4.1	16.6
Pacific Inter-Mountain Express	(39) Oakland	135,003	65,904	3,862	24,052	6,375	2.9	16.1
Yellow Freight System	(40) Kansas City	132,658	72,416	7,031	32,683	5,000	5.3	21.5
McLean Trucking	(44) Winston-Salem	113,861	64,263	5,217	26,520	6,194	4.6	19.7
Associated Transport	(47) New York	109,227	66,597	1,006	21,312	8,000	0.9	4.7
Spector Industries	(50) Chicago	97,691	51,955	186	11,986	4,887	n.a.	n.a.

Source: *Fortune*, Vol. LXXIX (May 15, 1969), pp. 196-197.

comes more apparent through an analysis of the distribution of revenue over a period of time. For example, in 1957 only one percent of the firms reporting had revenues over $10 million. These few firms, nevertheless, received 32.8 percent of all the revenues received by all the firms constituting the total population. By 1965, 2.5 percent of the reporting firms had revenues of $10 million or more and received 58.5 percent of all revenues.[17]

Industrial Location

The trucking industry covers the entire country, with corporate headquarters located primarily in urban centers, where most Negroes are concentrated. Table 4 is an array of the twenty-five largest SMSA's, showing Class I, II, and III carriers with corporate offices headquartered in these same twenty-five distinct geographical areas.

The most recent Negro population data on the basis of an SMSA are the statistics found in the 1960 census. Estimates have been made of the number of Negroes residing in the nation's larger cities (the heart of the SMSA's) rather than the SMSA proper. Projections for 1970 indicate that in the twenty-five cities included in Table 4, we should expect to find a total population of 31,671,000 people, of which 8,485,000 or 26.8 percent are Negroes.[18]

Included in the twenty-five SMSA's are 1,238 Class I and Class II carriers, or 36.5 percent of the total 3,397 such carriers found throughout the country in 1965. This then does not indicate where the industry is concentrated according to the gross revenue received from the particular markets it serves, nor does it reflect the number of employees found in each of these SMSA's. It does offer the opportunity to compare the industry geographically, and it also raises some questions as to why the firms' concentration pattern differs from area to area.

The concentration of large versus small companies in particular SMSA's is due to the geographical location of a particular SMSA in relationship to other markets and the density of each SMSA's population. For example, there are proportionately more

---

17. Interstate Commerce Commission, *81st Annual Report* (Washington: U.S. Government Printing Office, 1967), p. 152.

18. Cf. *The Negro Population: 1956 Estimates and 1970 Projections* (Peekskill: The Center of Research in Marketing, Incorporated).

TABLE 4. *For-Hire Carriers*
Location of Headquarters in Selected SMSA's
1966

SMSA by Size	Number of Carriers		
	Total	Class I and II Carriers	Class III Carriers
New York	397	119	278
Los Angeles	211	145	66
Chicago	307	153	154
Philadelphia	240	94	146
Detroit	74	54	20
San Francisco	96	61	35
Boston	172	65	107
Pittsburgh	127	61	66
St. Louis	116	59	57
Washington	33	15	18
Cleveland	79	43	36
Baltimore	63	26	37
Newark	110	36	74
Minneapolis-St. Paul	64	40	24
Buffalo	49	23	26
Houston	49	25	24
Milwaukee	57	33	24
Seattle	66	35	31
Dallas	41	26	15
Cincinnati	41	23	18
Kansas City	53	33	20
San Diego	10	6	4
Atlanta	29	20	9
Miami	19	8	11
Denver	67	35	32
Total	2,570	1,238	1,332

Source: *Trinc's Blue Book of the Trucking Industry* (1966 Edition), published annually by Trinc Associates, Ltd., Washington, D.C.

small carriers with headquarters in New York because of its position of centrality to many nearby markets. Conversely, there are more large carriers than small ones headquartered in Atlanta and Denver. Atlanta, the South's transportation hub, is a breaking point for shipments traveling the eastern coast and to the Midwest. In any case, the trucking industry has few locational problems relative to the Negro labor force.

MANPOWER

Table 5 shows that in 1966 the Class I and II carriers employed 573,304 people. Within the short span of nine years (1957-1966), the trucking industry increased its employment by 149,307, while the number of Class I and II carriers increased by 1,170. Although employment increased in absolute terms, the average number of employees per firm remained relatively constant.

TABLE 5.   *For-Hire Carriers*
Employment by Class
1957-1966

Year	Number of Class I and II Carriers[a]	Number of Employees	Average Number of Employees
1957	2,988	423,997	141.9
1958	3,155	415,859	131.8
1959	3,265	458,080	140.3
1960	3,329	466,726	140.2
1961	3,442	468,456	136.1
1962	3,643	509,656	140.0
1963	3,708	519,490	140.1
1964	3,731	534,279	143.2
1965	3,865	556,560	144.0
1966	4,158	573,304	137.9

Source: *American Trucking Trends, 1968* (Washington: American Trucking Associates, 1968), pp. 13 and 23.

[a] Included among these carriers are approximately 700 interstate carriers under ICC regulation with sufficient revenue to include them as Class I or II carriers.

Occupational Distribution

In sharp contrast to the relatively high ratio of white collar workers found in such industries as aerospace, only 25.6 percent of the trucking industry's employees, as Table 7 shows, are found in the white collar job category. The ratio of white collar workers in the trucking industry approximates what we find in such industries as paper and rubber tire. In the latter two, however, we find a smaller percentage of office and clerical employees. Only 10 percent of all trucking employees are found in occupations demanding more than a high school education. Consequently, we might assume that even with their disadvantaged educational status Negroes should find it relatively easy to secure employment in the majority of jobs available in the trucking industry. This is not the case, however, and why it is not so will be discussed in future chapters.

TABLE 6.   *Trucking Industry*
Employment by Occupation, 395 Class I Motor Carriers
1967

Occupational Group	Number of Employees	Percent of Total
Officials and Managers	21,004	7.7
Professionals	783	0.3
Technicians	975	0.4
Sales workers	6,298	2.3
Office and clerical	40,306	14.9
Total white collar	69,366	25.6
Craftsmen	20,553	7.6
Operatives	145,250	53.6
Laborers	32,066	11.8
Service workers	3,862	1.4
Total blue collar	201,731	74.4
Total	271,097	100.0

Source: Table 10, p. 37.

Under the heading of blue collar workers, we find that only 7.6 percent of all employees are craftsmen or skilled employees. Operatives, mostly the drivers, account for more than one-half of all employees. Although technically considered semiskilled, they frequently earn wages comparable to skilled workers in other industries. Although road drivers do not receive their training through formal apprenticeship programs, they have a tendency to view their occupation as a craft. They reserve these jobs for their friends and relatives, just as craft unions practice nepotism in accepting apprentices into their training programs. We should, therefore, expect to find that Negroes, in their effort to be employed as road drivers, must face some of the problems associated with being accepted in construction crafts.

Unionization

Since the mid-1930's, unionized long-haul motor carriers have had to contend with the International Brotherhood of Teamsters, at present the nation's largest union, and generally considered the most powerful one. In 1899, the American Federation of Labor granted a charter to the union, then known as the Teams Drivers International, permitting it to organize those driving horse-drawn carts. Over the years, the IBT expanded its jurisdiction and consequently its present membership [19] of approximately 1.6 million includes workers from such diverse industries as foundries, bakeries, airlines, undertaking establishments, and steel plants, as well as warehousing and trucking. An estimated 350,000 of the IBT's total membership are employed by trucking firms and these members belong to one of the union's sixteen trade divisions.

From 1900 to 1935, the vast majority of the IBT's members were employed as bread, laundry, milk, and ice and coal truck drivers. It is impossible to obtain precise data on the number of Negroes among the IBT's membership for this period. A Teamster representative stated that "probably" very few Negroes were members during these earlier years, unless they were originally

---

19. The Teamsters periodically issue official data on the number of dues-paying members. The "official" data are highly inflated. For example, the *International Teamster*, April 1968, maintained that the February membership was 1,911,212. The discrepancy between the 1.6 million figure used in this study and the "official" figure arises because dues-paying members are allowed to pay their dues on a quarterly basis. Therefore, if a man pays his dues for three months in January (for the first quarter of the year) he is counted as three members.

employed as helpers in the livery stables before the horse-drawn carts were replaced with trucks. There are several reasons why Negroes would not be found within the ranks of the Teamsters once the trucks replaced the horse-drawn carts.

First, although trucking was initially considered a Negro job in the South, Teamsters locals were concentrated in urban areas outside the South prior to 1935. Second, the bread, laundry, and milk drivers comprising the majority of the IBT's membership came in direct contact with the consumer as driver-salesmen, and anti-Negro sentiment often precluded their gaining admission to these jobs. Third, many IBT locals were dominated by distinct national and religious blocs which reserved these jobs for their own members. Fourth, although white strikebreakers outnumbered Negroes by more than seven to one, during the celebrated Teamsters strike of 1905 in Chicago, Negroes, because of their visibility, were blamed for taking the places of white men.[20] As a consequence, Negroes were prototyped as strikebreakers and much of this anti-Negro sentiment continued to exist over the years.

Most of the over-the-road drivers were brought into the Teamsters' Union in the 1930's. Prior to then, Daniel Tobin, longtime president of IBT, resisted organizing such "trash,"[21] but he was persuaded to change his views by the Troskyite Socialist, Farrell Dobbs, then head of the Minneapolis Teamsters. Dobbs, the organizational tutor of James Hoffa, used secondary boycotts and other leverage techniques to bring the bulk of the nation's over-the-road drivers into the union.[22] With the combination of over-the-road, local cartage, and warehouse workers into a single organization, the IBT is, as Mr. Hoffa has commented, very powerful.

Without the city cartage and the road organized in a territory . . . you cannot organize the rest of the city. Any employer who wants to fight you in any other branch of our business can whip the strongest local union unless you have the support of the road and city cartage. But once you organize the road, the city, the warehouses, nobody can whip the Teamsters union, nobody.[23]

---

20. Sterling D. Spero and Abram L. Harris, *The Black Worker* (New York: Atheneum, 1968), p. 132.

21. Ralph C. James and Estelle Dinerstein James, *Hoffa and the Teamsters* (New York: D. Van Nostrand Co., Inc., 1965), p. 91.

22. *Ibid.*, Chapters 5 and 6.

23. *Ibid.*, p. 57.

The over-the-road drivers did not alter the prevailing attitude
of the IBT toward Negroes. As craft conscious as the local
salesmen-drivers, they also saw their members displace lower-
paid blacks after southern firms were organized. Because of the
significance of the Teamsters in the industry, we shall deal with
its policies in depth in succeeding chapters.

Future Employment Needs

There are no indications that recent increases in productivity,
and new adaptations, such as containerization,[24] will compel the
trucking industry to decrease its demand for labor. If anything,
the trucking industry is one of the nation's growth industries and
should continue to offer jobs requiring a minimal amount of
formal education and/or training; jobs that disadvantaged persons, many of whom are Negroes, should be able to fill.

Between 1961 and 1965, line drivers increased the tons hauled
per man-hour by 2.6 percent, while the miles per man-hour increased by 1.1 percent. Moreover, pickup and delivery drivers
increased the tons per mile they hauled by 1.5 percent. Platform
employees increased the tons per man-hour they handled by 1.1
percent.[25] These increases in tons and miles per man-hour are
indicative of the industry's ability to adapt to new technologies
and to use more efficiently their manpower resources.

As a percentage of GNP, the nation's total freight bill has decreased, while the percentage of revenues received by the trucking industry has increased. That is, as the total freight bill as
a percentage of GNP decreased from 9.2 percent in 1958 to 8.9
percent in 1964, the trucking freight bill, for the same period,
increased from 5.9 to 6.3 percent. Of greater significance is the
fact that in 1964 all trucking accounted for 71.2 percent of total
freight service, while the projected 1980 figure is 78.6 percent.[26]
Therefore, productivity increases in trucking should be more
than offset by the industry's growth, and demand for labor in
absolute terms should increase.

Motor freight transportation and warehousing industries are
expected to increase their manpower requirements by one-fifth,

---

24. For details about some of the limitations in containerization, see *Wall
Street Journal*, May 28, 1968, p. 34.

25. Unpublished data made available by the American Trucking Associations, Inc.

26. Edward V. Kiley, "Looking Ahead," *Trucking and the Economy* (Washington: American Trucking Associations, Inc., 1966), pp. 26-28.

rising to approximately 1.2 million, between 1966 and 1975.[27] Although we can expect 129,000 truck driver openings annually through 1975,[28] intercity motor carriers are not expected to expand in the future as rapidly as they did in the past. Local driver openings should increase annually at the rate of 74,000, while over-the-road drivers should increase at the annual rate of 55,000 through 1975. The demand for local drivers should increase more rapidly than that of over-the-road drivers because of an increase in the number of suburban shopping centers, and as a result of industry relocating away from the center city areas.

The greatest employment growth is expected to occur among larger firms which, compared to smaller companies, have a higher proportion of professional workers, clerical workers, mechanics and repairmen, and foremen. In the past, the ratio of sales workers to all other workers has been relatively low. Demand for salesmen, however, is expected to rise appreciably over the next decade as competition from other modes of transportation, in particular air carriers, increases. Computer usage might well tend to moderate the growth rates of clerical positions that should increase as the industry expands.

Of basic importance to the employment of the Negro is the fact that the demand for blue collar workers is increasing within the trucking industry. From 1961 to 1966, all blue collar jobs throughout the nation increased at an annual rate of 700,000, but in 1967 the increase was only 300,000.[29] Therefore, unlike the steel industry [30] where job opportunities are being phased out by new technologies, and unlike the aerospace industry [31] where

27. U.S. Bureau of Labor Statistics, *Tomorrow's Manpower Needs*, Vol. II, Bulletin No. 1606 (Washington: U.S. Government Printing Office, 1969), pp. 83-85.

28. U.S. Bureau of Labor Statistics, *Occupational Outlook Quarterly*, Vol. 12, No. 2, May 1968 (Washington: U.S. Government Printing Office), p. 6. Annual average openings are those jobs arising because of growth, death and retirement losses. It does not include transfers out of the occupation. A shortage of dependable drivers exists in New York City. For details, see *Wall Street Journal*, November 11, 1969, p. 1.

29. *Wall Street Journal*, June 4, 1968, p. 1.

30. Herbert R. Northrup *et al.*, *Negro Employment in Basic Industry*, Negro Employment Studies, Vol. I (Philadelphia: Industrial Research Unit, Wharton School of Finance and Commerce, University of Pennsylvania, 1970), Part Four.

31. *Ibid.*, Part Three.

many jobs are highly skilled, the motor freight industry is increasing its demand for blue collar workers. Although road drivers view their occupation as a craft, there are no formal procedures a man must follow to learn how to drive. When truck manufacturers incorporate new improvements into the trucks, most drivers can learn how to operate these vehicles without a great deal of formal training. Consequently, Negroes who may suffer from such handicaps as poor education should in the future find this a relatively easy industry in which to find employment. But this possibility must be viewed in light of some of the obstacles Negroes have found in the past, which we will discuss in subsequent chapters.

CHAPTER III

Negro Employment Prior to 1960

Prior to 1960, Negroes employed in over-the-road trucking were found mostly in the South. Particularly before World War II, and in the postwar years as well, as noted in Chapter II, many of the trucking firms were small, family-owned and managed concerns. Consequently, their hiring procedures were very informal. The smaller firms relied on friends and relatives to meet their needs. The larger firms, with terminals located throughout the country, usually relied on recommendations from their present employees in hiring new ones. Negroes employed in the South were hired largely by nonunion firms whose ·wages were low and hours and working conditions substandard.

Table 7 shows the number of Negroes employed from 1940 to 1960 by the trucking and warehousing industries and the percentage of the work force they represented, with breakdowns for males and females and four geographical regions. A word of caution is called for, however, because these census statistics represent racial employment patterns not only for trucking, but also for warehousing. Compared to the range of jobs available in the trucking industry, warehousing offers jobs of less status and relatively poorer pay. If the statistics shown on Table 7 were for trucking alone, rather than warehousing and trucking, it is safe to assume that the number of Negroes employed would be somewhat lower. Furthermore, the methodology used in collecting census data (personal interview) suggests that private carrier employers are included in the statistics as reported.

From 1940 to 1960, the proportion of Negro employment in trucking and warehousing increased only by five-tenths of a percentage point. Although male Negro employment increased from 7.6 percent in 1940 to 8.3 percent in 1960, female Negro employment, during the same period, remained relatively constant. The South accounted for the largest percentage of Negroes, but the ratio of Negroes decreased there, while the percentage of Negroes increased in the Northeast and West and remained relatively stable in the Midwest. It is likely that, in fact, Negroes lost jobs in trucking in the South and gained warehousing jobs in other areas.

TABLE 7. *Trucking and Warehousing Industry Employment by Race and Sex United States and Regions, 1940-1960*

Region	Year	All Employees			Male			Female		
		Total	Negro	Percent Negro	Total	Negro	Percent Negro	Total	Negro	Percent Negro
United States	1940	488,816	36,210	7.4	470,023	35,698	7.6	18,793	512	2.7
	1950	696,165	50,373	7.2	649,247	48,709	7.5	46,918	1,664	3.5
	1960	841,418	66,243	7.9	774,621	64,477	8.3	66,797	1,766	2.6
Northeast	1940	137,221	5,858	4.3	131,739	5,756	4.4	5,482	102	1.9
	1950	183,835	9,593	5.2	171,915	9,279	5.4	11,920	314	2.6
	1960	205,536	14,327	6.9	191,206	13,879	7.3	14,330	448	3.1
Midwest	1940	174,159	4,042	2.3	167,065	3,980	2.4	7,094	62	0.9
	1950	251,088	8,019	3.2	234,042	7,605	3.2	17,046	414	2.4
	1960	298,288	8,764	2.9	273,561	8,405	3.1	24,727	359	1.5
South	1940	122,763	25,712	20.9	119,206	25,372	21.3	3,557	340	9.6
	1950	171,325	30,903	18.0	161,116	30,071	18.7	10,209	832	8.1
	1960	206,826	40,113	19.4	190,898	39,245	20.6	15,928	868	5.4
West	1940	54,673	598	1.1	52,013	589	1.1	2,660	8	0.3
	1950	89,917	1,858	2.1	82,174	1,754	2.1	7,743	104	1.3
	1960	130,768	3,039	2.3	118,956	2,948	2.5	11,812	91	0.8

Source: *U.S. Census of Population:*

1940: Vol. III, *The Labor Force*, Part I, Table 77.

1950: Vol. II, *Characteristics of the Population*, Table 161.

1960: PC (1) 1D, *Detailed Characteristics*, Table 260.

Note: Regions are defined as follows:

Northeast: Connecticut, Maine, Massachusetts, New Hampshire, New Jersey, New York, Pennsylvania, Rhode Island, Vermont.

Midwest: Illinois, Indiana, Iowa, Kansas, Michigan, Minnesota, Missouri, Nebraska, North Dakota, Ohio, South Dakota, Wisconsin.

South: Alabama, Arkansas, Delaware, Florida, Georgia, Kentucky, Louisiana, Maryland, Mississippi, North Carolina, Oklahoma, South Carolina, Tennessee, Texas, Virginia, West Virginia.

West: Arizona, California, Colorado, Idaho, Montana, Nevada, New Mexico, Oregon, Utah, Washington, Wyoming (Hawaii and Alaska included 1960).

SOCIAL INFLUENCES

Prior to the passage of the Civil Rights Act of 1964, Negroes were often refused admission to places offering public lodging. Employers, especially those with terminals in the South, contend that this was the primary reason why they did not hire Negro road drivers. Since the amount and nature of freight crossing terminal thresholds varies from day to day, truckers must have the freedom to assign drivers. To have as road drivers Negroes who would be unable to accept certain trips because they could not find public accommodations, would have deprived the employers of the flexibility they needed in assigning drivers to different runs.

On long trips, more than one driver is assigned to the job, with one driver sleeping in a cab-bunk, or the drivers sharing rooms en route. Custom and belief made white drivers extremely adverse to having a black "buddy"—a factor still militating against Negro employment today.

Many of the black road drivers found today working for trucking companies were hired during World War II, when the union and employers were compelled by the tight labor markets to admit some Negroes into these high-paying jobs. Even so, tight labor markets did not operate as favorably for Negroes in trucking as they did in some other industries from which they had been excluded prior to World War II. According to Leiter:

More Negroes were employed, especially in the South, but even greater absorption of this group would have been possible if company and union discrimination had not been practiced. The labor needs of the trucking industry were mostly for replacements. Labor shortages experienced by the industry in each community corresponded with the inadequacy of the general labor supply in that geographical area.[32]

Thus, during World War II and the years thereafter, Negro gains in trucking remained quite limited. Like railroad firemen, they were used in the South as a source of cheap labor, but such usage declined as southern wages rose. In other parts of the country, the trucking industry's stance on Negro employment was similar to that of other industrial segments in transportation— railroad, airlines, and shipping companies. The most prestigious jobs of airline flight officer and maritime vessel officer, or rail-

---

32. Robert D. Leiter, *The Teamsters Union* (New York: Bookman Associates, 1957), p. 145.

road engineer and conductor remained virtually all white. The highly paid, but less prestigious, over-the-road truck operators had only a few Negroes in their ranks. And particularly like the railroad situation, the decision to maintain Negro employment at a minimum was, over the years, strongly influenced by union policy and structure representing the institutionalized prejudices of the white employees.[33]

TEAMSTER INFLUENCE

Prior to the election of James Hoffa as Teamster president in the late 1950's, the union was operated as a confederation of highly independent locals and conferences.[34] Daniel Tobin, president from 1908 to 1952, was content to permit maximum local autonomy. If a local, therefore, wished to confine its members to whites, Tobin did not make it the concern of the national office. As a matter of fact, if Tobin's own preference had been influential, the results would not have been salutary for Negroes. One of the current union officials stated, in a confidential interview: "Tobin did not like Italians, Jews, or Negroes; as a matter of fact, the only people he did like were Irish Catholics." [35] Tobin's attitude, and those of many of the officers of local unions, exemplified the craft conscious, work scarcity feelings found in the building trades unions.[36] The milk, bread, and other salesmen-driver locals were traditionally white and their customer contact jobs increased their white collar, as well as craft, orientation. Over-the-road drivers added their club-like feelings to the group, all of whom felt that Negroes had little or no place in their midst.

---

33. Howard W. Risher, Jr., *The Negro in the Railroad Industry*, The Racial Policies of American Industry, Report No. 16 (Philadelphia: Industrial Research Unit, Wharton School of Finance and Commerce, University of Pennsylvania, 1970).

34. The area conferences, four in number, came upon the scene as area agreements expanded to include several states under the contracts. The Western Conference includes eleven western states. The Eastern Conference is confined to the states along the Atlantic coast as far South, and including, the Carolinas. The Central and Southern Conferences include those states indicated by their very titles.

35. Interview, 1965.

36. See, for example, Herbert R. Northrup, *Organized Labor and the Negro* (New York: Harper and Brothers, 1944), Chapter II.

Given these feelings, it is likely that Tobin clearly reflected the feelings of his membership toward Negroes. Even if he did not, however, local autonomy in the union was so pronounced that it is doubtful if Tobin could have done much to insure Negro employment even if he had so desired.

Under David Beck, president of the Teamsters from 1952 through 1958, the union's structure and posture toward Negroes encountered little change. Local autonomy prevailed, and action toward improved Negro employment opportunity was largely nonexistent. Beck, on a number of occasions, did place locals under national trusteeship (indeed, his propensity to do this was a factor in regulating such activity when Congress enacted the Landrum-Griffin Act of 1959), suspending local officers, and instructing his trustees to admit to membership all applicants into those locals. Allegedly this was done because he viewed it as a means of weakening the political machine controlling the local, not because he was an egalitarian reformer. If, through custom, some employment opportunities were considered "Negro jobs," such as taxicab drivers in the South who provided services for Negroes only, segregated locals provided union services for these members.[37]

When James R. Hoffa succeeded to the Teamsters presidency, he had acquired a reputation of being more interested in Negro support and Negro rights. His prime goals, however, appeared to be the consolidation of power to the national presidency at the expense of the locals and conferences, and, as part of this program, the signing of a national trucking agreement. He therefore seemed to view the enlargement of Negro membership in the union only in relation to its effects upon his prime goals. Hoffa's objectives and the internal political climate of the union, therefore, tended to relegate Negro rights approximately the same low status that they occupied during previous Teamster presidents' administrations.[38]

We may sum up this brief review by noting that there was little or no pressure from the top of the Teamsters' Union for

---

37. A discussion of Beck's attitudes and philosophy is found in Donald Garnel, "Teamsters and Highway Truckers in the West—The Evaluation of Multiemployer Bargaining in the Western Trucking Industry," unpublished Ph.D. dissertation, University of California, Berkeley, 1966; and Sam Romer, *The International Brotherhood of Teamsters: Its Government and Structure* (New York: John Wiley and Sons, Inc., 1962).

38. See Romer, *op. cit.*, and James, *op. cit.*, *passim.*

nondiscriminatory practices during the period covered. On the contrary, the pressures in favor of discrimination in the locals were largely uninhibited. Even the union's constitution was, during this period, and remains today, equivocal. It provides:

Any person shall be eligible to membership in this organization, provided that hereafter no person shall be eligible for membership in the International Union who has willfully refused to become a citizen of either the United States or Canada or the country in which his Local Union is chartered, at his option.[39]

Union constitutions prohibiting the exclusion of members because of race, color, or creed are certainly no guarantee that a union is truly fair in admitting members. Even so, the Teamsters' constitution, which states that any person shall be eligible, does not allude to race, color, or creed. During Beck's regime, Teamster officials discussed whether specific mention should be made about the union's willingness to accept everyone regardless of race, color, or creed. This change was never made, on the assumption that if it were changed, it might be interpreted to mean that the union had been guilty of discrimination over the years. Therefore, to the degree that such explicit nondiscriminatory eligibility clauses found in other union constitutions are of any value, it is well to note that the Teamsters constitution was —and is—silent on this point.

During the latter part of Tobin's regime, and in more recent years, the Teamsters' Union has aggressively organized employees—first in warehouses, then in a variety of industries wherever it could obtain members. Many of the nontrucking firms organized by the Teamsters (including those in the South where the union is apparently growing the fastest) employ considerably more Negroes than do the motor carriers. In such cases the union has often adopted a pro-black stance, utilizing Negro organizers where it deems them effective. Yet in the key industry—public interstate trucking—the union has few Negro members and has demonstrated little zeal in altering this situation. Moreover, it is the over-the-road truckers on which the Teamsters union relies to assist in organizing other industries. Within the union, therefore, this group is the most powerful, politically and economically. Union officials have been reluctant to advocate positive programs for equal employment because they

---

39. International Brotherhood of Teamsters, Chauffeurs, Warehousemen and Helpers of America, *Constitution*, 1966, Article II, Section 2(a).

could affect this internal balance of power. In turn, the industry has been compelled to negotiate collective bargaining agreements with a formidable foe and is not anxious to make changes
in work rules, seniority rights, and changes in their operations
that might in any way grant the union a competitive advantage
at the bargaining table. To what extent this status quo has been
affected by developments of the 1960's, including especially the
Civil Rights legislation and activity of that period and the new
leadership of the Teamsters' Union, will be discussed in the following chapters.

CHAPTER IV

Negro Employment in the 1960's

The trucking industry entered the decade of the 1960's with few Negro over-the-road drivers. The data developed for this chapter show that this pattern had not changed significantly by 1968. Why the institutional factors limiting Negro employment proved too difficult to overcome is discussed in this and subsequent chapters after a review of the data.

THE OVERALL PICTURE

Employment in motor freight transportation and warehousing by race, sex, and broad occupational group was reported on by the Equal Employment Opportunity Commission in 1966 (Table 8). Like the 1960 census data, the EEOC compilation includes warehouse employees as well as truckers. Unfortunately the EEOC and census data are not strictly comparable. The former is based upon reports from employers of 100 or more, whereas the latter is the result of responses of individuals to interviewers. Thus, the census includes drivers of companies with less than 100 employees and undoubtedly drivers working for private carriers, plus any discrepancies resulting from differences in how individuals view themselves as compared with how they are viewed by their employers.

Nevertheless, the significant fact is the closeness of the results. In 1960, the census found (Table 7 above) that 7.9 percent of those in trucking and warehouses were Negroes, with a male ratio of 8.3 percent and a female one of 2.6 percent. Table 8 lists EEOC results as 6.3 percent Negro overall, 6.6 male and 2.3 percent female. Allowing for differences resulting from the different statistical and sampling methods, it would appear that Negroes made no progress, or were actually set back, in the first half of the 1960's.

A comparison of the employment data reported to the EEOC in 1966 by the motor carrier and warehousing industries with the data submitted by all industries or manufacturing industries

TABLE 8. *Motor Freight Transportation and Warehousing (SIC 42)*
Employment by Race, Sex, and Occupational Group
United States, 1966

Occupational Group	All Employees			Male			Female		
	Total	Negro	Percent Negro	Total	Negro	Percent Negro	Total	Negro	Percent Negro
Officials and managers	30,728	127	0.4	30,060	121	0.4	668	6	0.9
Professionals	2,353	17	0.7	2,272	17	0.7	81	—	—
Technicians	921	25	2.7	867	23	2.7	54	2	3.7
Sales workers	8,245	56	0.7	8,016	50	0.6	229	6	2.6
Office and clerical	55,026	582	1.1	25,394	315	1.2	29,632	267	0.9
Total white collar	97,273	807	0.8	66,609	526	0.8	30,664	281	0.9
Craftsmen	34,424	1,736	5.0	34,331	1,733	5.0	93	3	3.2
Operatives	198,228	11,313	5.7	197,798	11,265	5.7	430	48	11.2
Laborers	53,044	8,929	16.8	51,835	8,635	16.7	1,209	294	24.3
Service workers	7,394	1,632	22.1	7,115	1,493	21.0	279	139	49.8
Total blue collar	293,090	23,610	8.1	291,079	23,126	7.9	2,011	484	24.1
Total	390,363	24,417	6.3	357,688	23,652	6.6	32,675	765	2.3

Source: Equal Employment Opportunity Commission, *Job Patterns for Minorities and Women in Private Industry, 1966,* Report No. 1 (Washington: The Commission, 1968), Part II.

Note: For a definition of SIC 42, see Figure 2, p. 6.

alone, reveals that the former's white-Negro employment ratio is lower than that reported by either all industries or manufacturing industries (Table 9). For example, only 0.8 percent of all white collar workers employed by the trucking and warehousing industries were Negroes, while all industries reported that 2.6 percent of their white collar workers were Negroes, and manufacturing industries reported that 1.2 percent of their white collar workers were Negroes. A similar differential arises when we assess the employment statistics compiled under the blue collar classification. Also, the ratio of the Negroes employed as service workers is high for the three industrial groups listed in Table 9. Thus, the trucking and warehousing industries in 1966 employed more Negroes as service workers than did manufacturing industries, but they employed slightly less percentagewise than that reported by all industries. The varied circumstances and factors which have caused these divergent racial employment profiles to arise will be discussed in subsequent chapters.

The 1967 Sample

We have already noted that if statistics were available for trucking alone, the proportion of Negroes would be less than that for trucking and warehousing combined. Data set forth in Table 10, covering 395 Class I motor carriers for 1967, substantiate this. Only 4.5 percent in this sample are black, as compared with 6.3 percent in Table 9. This table also points up the concentration of Negroes in the lower job classifications. Less than one percent of the salaried workers were black, as were only 3.7 percent of the craftsmen and 4.6 of the operatives. On the other hand, 10.7 percent of the laborers and 23 percent of the service workers were Negroes. Although Table 8 shows the same wide representation of Negroes in white collar employment, it does show a better representation of Negroes in the top two blue collar classifications, although an even greater concentration of Negroes as laborers. Overall, it would appear that Negroes are not only better represented in warehousing than trucking, but have had better opportunities in the top blue collar jobs in the former as well.

The data in Table 10 are, of course, from the larger Class I carriers only and it is possible that the smaller firms employ a larger percentage of Negroes. In addition, the occupational groups in Table 9 are more suitable to manufacturing than to transportation employment. In an unpublished study made avail-

TABLE 9. *Motor Freight Transportation and Warehousing (SIC 42)*
Compared with All Industries and Manufacturing Industries
Employment by Race, Sex, and Occupational Group
Total United States, 1966

Occupational Group	All Industries			Manufacturing Industries			Motor Freight Transportation and Warehousing		
	Total	Negro	Percent Negro	Total	Negro	Percent Negro	Total	Negro	Percent Negro
Officials and managers	2,077,663	18,106	0.9	878,497	4,991	0.6	30,728	127	0.4
Professionals	1,689,886	22,333	1.3	670,818	3,732	0.6	2,353	17	0.7
Technicians	1,137,952	46,503	4.1	448,217	6,563	1.5	921	25	2.7
Sales workers	1,796,574	42,417	2.4	346,136	4,160	1.2	8,245	56	0.7
Office and clerical	4,264,770	151,105	3.5	1,307,982	26,193	2.0	55,026	582	1.1
Total white collar	10,966,845	280,464	2.6	3,651,650	45,639	1.2	97,273	807	0.8
Craftsmen	3,626,470	130,543	3.6	2,199,536	82,343	3.7	34,424	1,736	5.0
Operatives	6,499,351	702,234	10.8	5,020,500	531,586	10.6	198,228	11,313	5.7
Laborers	2,465,901	523,970	21.2	1,623,100	297,509	18.3	53,044	8,929	16.8
Service workers	1,952,135	452,036	23.2	247,082	53,521	21.7	7,394	1,632	22.1
Total blue collar	14,543,857	1,808,783	12.4	9,090,218	964,959	10.6	293,090	23,610	8.1
Total	25,510,702	2,089,247	8.2	13,741,868	1,010,598	7.4	390,363	24,417	6.3

Source: Equal Employment Opportunity Commission, *Job Patterns for Minorities and Women in Private Industry, 1966,* Report No. 1 (Washington: The Commission, 1968), Part II.

Note: For a definition of SIC 42, see Figure 2, p. 6. Table does not include Alaska and Hawaii.

TABLE 10. *Trucking Industry*
Employment by Race, Sex, and Occupational Group
395 Class I Motor Carriers
1967

Occupational Group	All Employees			Male			Female		
	Total	Negro	Percent Negro	Total	Negro	Percent Negro	Total	Negro	Percent Negro
Officials and managers	21,004	54	0.3	20,616	53	0.3	388	1	0.3
Professionals	783	1	0.1	742	1	0.1	41	—	—
Technicians	975	2	0.2	955	2	0.2	20	—	—
Sales workers	6,298	3	0.1	6,229	3	0.1	69	—	—
Office and clerical	40,306	348	0.8	17,945	144	0.8	22,361	204	0.9
Total white collar	69,366	408	0.6	46,437	203	0.4	22,879	205	0.9
Craftsmen	20,553	762	3.7	20,547	762	3.7	6	—	—
Operatives	145,290	6,709	4.6	145,241	6,707	4.6	9	2	22.2
Laborers	32,006	3,537	10.7	32,040	3,534	10.7	26	3	11.5
Service workers	3,862	889	23.0	3,695	829	22.4	167	60	35.9
Total blue collar	201,731	11,897	5.9	201,523	11,832	5.9	208	65	31.2
Total	271,097	12,305	4.5	248,010	12,035	4.9	23,087	270	1.2

Source: Data in author's possession.

able to the author for 1967, seventeen carriers were found to employ 10,639 road drivers, of whom only 71, or 0.7 percent were black.[40] This would seem to corroborate both the lack of representation of Negroes as drivers and their concentration in lower-paid jobs.

The 1968 Field Sample

In order to examine the Negro employment situation more thoroughly, a careful field study was made in 1968 of a selected sample of large and small carriers in forty-eight metropolitan areas.[41] These data are set forth in Table 11 by occupations found in the trucking industry.

Negroes comprise 7.6 percent of the labor force of these firms, as compared with the 4.5 percent of the ratio for 395 Class I carriers in 1967 (Table 10). Allowing for some increase in the employment of Negroes between 1967 and 1968, the difference is both substantial and easily explained. The data in Table 10 are comparable to those for large firms in Table 11. The latter has a Negro proportion of 5.7 percent, higher than the figure for the 395 Class I carriers, but possibly attributable to the stringencies of the labor market in 1968 over 1967 for lower-rated jobs.

On the other hand, in the smaller firms included in this sample, 11.3 percent of the employees and 5.3 percent of the road drivers were black. Only 0.9 percent of the large company drivers were Negroes. Because the work is distasteful and difficult in some of these smaller companies, Negroes find it easier to find employment with them, for example, as brick movers and household movers. Also, small nonunion firms, particularly in the South, traditionally employ a larger number of Negroes.

For both large and small firms, the data in Table 10 corroborate those in previous tables in so far as occupational distribution is concerned. Except for the local drivers, 50 percent of the Negroes in the sample are employed in the lower pay and lower status jobs, such as docksmen, oilers, washers, service workers, and helpers. The more prestigious occupation of driver, seemingly unattainable to large numbers of Negro workers, demands a more detailed examination.

---

40. Data in author's possession.

41. Small firms consist of Class I and II carriers employing 100 or less hourly employees. See Appendix A and B for methodology.

TABLE 11. Trucking Industry
Employment by Race, Occupation, and Company Size
United States, 1968

Job Classifications	All Firms			Small Firms[a]			Large Firms[b]		
	Total	Negro	Percent Negro	Total	Negro	Percent Negro	Total	Negro	Percent Negro
Management	14,337	13	0.1	4,753	—	—	9,584	13	0.1
Road drivers	59,887	1,417	2.4	19,669	1,037	5.3	40,218	380	0.9
Local drivers	53,920	5,865	10.9	25,602	3,977	15.5	28,318	1,888	6.7
Dockmen	31,336	3,968	12.7	5,914	1,702	28.8	25,422	2,266	8.9
Mechanics	13,051	775	5.9	3,376	179	5.3	9,675	596	6.2
Oilers	354	231	65.3	22	22	100.0	332	209	63.0
Washers	849	786	92.6	206	206	100.0	643	580	90.2
Service workers	2,564	1,115	43.5	451	301	66.7	2,113	814	38.5
Dispatchers	4,270	8	0.2	1,575	—	—	2,695	8	0.3
Warehousemen	706	100	14.2	412	43	10.4	294	57	19.4
Helpers	6,559	1,239	18.9	4,062	619	15.2	2,497	620	24.8
Clerical workers	23,406	538	2.3	5,473	—	—	17,933	538	3.0
Total	211,239	16,055	7.6	71,515	8,086	11.3	139,724	7,969	5.7

Source: Data in author's possession.

Note: See Appendix A for details of sample selection and Appendix B for the methodology used to adjust the original data for this and subsequent tables.

[a] Small firms are those having 100 or less employees.

[b] Large firms are those having 101 or more employees.

THE ROAD DRIVERS

The Motor Carrier Act of 1935 established safety regulations which forced employers to be more exacting in the employment of interstate drivers. These regulations, and their subsequent modifications over the years, not only compel a potential driver to meet specific health requirements, but to be familiar with the rules and regulations associated with safe driving.[42] In addition, each state has rules governing licenses for commercial drivers which very from state to state.

Driver Qualifications

Although the Department of Transportation's regulations stipulate that a long-haul driver must be at least twenty-one years old, most employers insist that they be older. This age requirement varies from firm to firm, but the average minimal age among the firms interviewed was twenty-six. Regardless of a firm's size, nature, or locale, the companies argue that a man below this minimal age is not mature enough to assume the responsibility for a piece of equipment valued at $35,000, containing commodities sometimes worth well over $100,000.

The over-the-road driver must be able to drive safely a gasoline or today's more popular diesel-powered tractor, which with the loaded trailers are difficult to handle. In addition to meeting the age requirement, the Department of Transportation compels a potential over-the-road driver to pass a physical examination and, in the larger firms, to take a written examination to demonstrate his knowledge of safety rules and regulations. The applicant must also be able to speak and write English because a driver must keep a daily log of his road activities, and, in case of an accident, must file a detailed report. Besides being capable of handling the various types of vehicles operated by the hiring firm, the applicant must have a satisfactory driving record and he should have no criminal record. These latter two requirements often are used by employers as reasons for not hiring Negroes as road drivers. Yet, some firms use a very narrow

---

42. For more details, see U.S. Department of Transportation, Federal Highway Administration, Bureau of Motor Carrier Safety, *Motor Carrier Safety Regulations* (Washington: U.S. Government Printing Office, 1968). For a discussion of proposed revision of the safety regulations and the Teamsters objection to same, see "Federal Highway Commission Revising Driver Qualifications," *The International Teamster*, Vol. 60, No. 9 (September 1969), pp. 15-16.

definition of what constitutes a criminal record, while others will refuse to hire the man only if the criminal charge has been serious and recent.

Over and above the health and safety regulations spelled out by the Department of Transportation, there are also standards established by the industry, primarily by custom. Virtually all firms, regardless of size or geographical location, will not hire a driver for an over-the-road opening unless he has had approximately three years' experience driving a tractor trailer, including some experience under conditions comparable to those he should encounter in his new job. As subsequent analyses will demonstrate, one of the real obstacles faced by Negroes in being employed as line-haul drivers is the employers' contention that they lack sufficient experience as drivers.

With prior experience a necessary condition of employment, some of the larger firms sponsor and finance their own training programs, and pay the trainee according to a graduated pay schedule. One firm, sponsoring what is considered by many employers at the best training program in the country, prefers that the trainee not have driven a truck for any other motor carrier firm. Second, there are private truck driver training schools throughout the country, some costing as much as $800. As a rule, employers are not satisfied with the graduates of these schools, and are reluctant to hire them. In practice, most over-the-road drivers enter the occupation by first driving a small truck as a local driver for private or public carriers; then after gaining experience, they move to the larger and more complicated vehicles. Some gain entrance into the driving occupation by working as helpers with local truck drivers.

Drivers employed by public carriers frequently start on the "extra board," bidding for regular runs on the basis of seniority as vacancies occur. The extra board consists of a rotating list of drivers who substitute for regular drivers when they are on vacation, or who make extra trips when the demand for truck transportation increases. The seasonal variations in truck transportation are caused by holiday buying patterns and by peak periods of stocking merchandise. As a general rule, Monday and Friday are the carriers' busiest days of the week because neither they nor the shippers want merchandise tied up on platforms over the weekend. The extra board and the use of casual drivers enable the employer to use his labor force more flexibly as the demand for truck services changes.

The seemingly objective requirements stated above must be viewed in conjunction with personal demands made on over-the-road drivers.[43] They must be willing to spend time away from home. Senior drivers, who are able to bid on the better-paying runs, have been known to spend as many as 250 nights per year sleeping in the cab of a tractor trailer or in dormitory facilities provided by the employer at distant terminals.

On extremely long runs, a two-man sleeper team is operative; one man drives while the other sleeps in the bunk behind the cab. Normally, a driver on such a team may choose his driving partner. Most IBT contracts grant over-the-road drivers the right to choose new driving partners annually. The duration of these "marriages," as they are referred to, depends on the ability of the men to work together in such close quarters and the existence of this arrangement adds to the reluctance of employers to hire Negro road drivers.

When sleeper teams are used, they travel nonstop to a terminal location where the freight is delivered to receivers in the area by local drivers using smaller trucks, and the driver has a layover before the return trip. During the actual trip, moreover, the driver has two four-hour periods of sleep or rest in the berth of the truck. This meets the Department of Transportation's regulation which calls for eight hours off duty following ten hours of driving. Even so, under these conditions a team of drivers may remain away from the base terminal for seventy hours during an eight-day period, often making two or three such round trips a week.

Over-the-road driving is well paid. Wages range from $10,000 to $20,000 per year, with the average annual wage in the neighborhood of $11,500 per year. Given the lack of formal education required, the jobs do attract capable people. Negroes desiring such work find considerable white worker competition for the jobs.

Negro Availability

Approximately 90 percent of the companies interviewed suggested that they were more than willing to hire Negroes as over-the-road drivers as long as qualified Negroes applied. They emphatically stated that if the federal government or any of the

---

43. See Ross A. McFarland and Alfred L. Moseley, *Human Factors in Highway Transport Safety* (Boston: Harvard School of Public Health, 1955).

several city and state agencies would just produce one qualified Negro road driver, they would hire him tomorrow. At the same time they argued that morality cannot be legislated, and as a group they seemed insensitive to that nebulous idealization labeled "corporate responsibility." Thus, the companies generally fear hiring marginal employees because of the cost involved, and they refuse to lower their hiring standards. In practice, however, only the giant firms in the industry employ hiring procedures that are somewhat consistent and seemingly equitable. Most of the others seemed to assume that all Negroes are marginal and unqualified.

The real test of the companies' contention that they cannot find qualified Negro road drivers is in determining whether or not the nation's labor markets do in fact contain Negroes who would meet the government's requirements and the companies' standards. The record demonstrates that the Post Office Department does find qualified Negroes to fill openings arising among their road drivers who perform the same tasks as do drivers of trucking companies.

Table 13 shows the total number and percentage of Negroes employed as tractor trailer and motor vehicle operators by the Post Office within the SMSA's that comprise this study's sample labor markets. Although representatives from the private carriers argue that competent Negro road drivers cannot be found, the statistics indicate that, of the tractor trailer drivers employed by the Post Office Department, 553 or 62.3 percent are Negroes. When other motor vehicle operators, who substitute when necessary for tractor trailer operators, are included, the percentage of Negroes is 60.5. The type of equipment used, the work setting, and the basic occupational requirements existing at these various Post Office locations are identical to that found in the private sector of the economy. It would appear that the inadequate supply argument used by the trucking industry is not supported by the evidence.

Supervisory personnel working for the POD who were interviewed by the author report that the Negroes' absenteeism, lateness, and turnover rates are no higher than those prevailing among white employees. On the other hand, public carriers without any Negro road drivers suggested in interviews that Negroes are in short supply and, as a group, are not dependable. This all-pervading attitude is difficult to evaluate in quantifiable terms, but these biases are apparently harbored by many em-

TABLE 12. *Tractor Trailer and Motor Vehicle Operators*
Post Office Department Employment by Race
Selected SMSA's, 1968

SMSA[a]	Tractor Trailer and Motor Vehicle Operators[b]			Tractor Trailer Operators[b]			Motor Vehicle Operators[b]		
	Total	Negro	Percent Negro	Total	Negro	Percent Negro	Total	Negro	Percent Negro
Atlanta	27	18	66.7	27	18	66.7	—	—	—
Boston	89	12	13.5	38	5	13.2	51	7	13.7
Chicago	296	200	67.6	197	120	60.9	99	80	80.8
Detroit	49	43	87.8	16	14	87.5	33	29	87.9
Dallas	11	6	54.5	11	6	54.5	—	—	—
Denver[c]	1	—	—	1	—	—	—	—	—
New York	377	210	55.7	367	204	55.6	10	6	60.0
Philadelphia	87	73	83.9	31	27	87.1	56	46	82.1
St. Louis	144	58	40.3	35	25	71.4	109	33	30.3
San Francisco	71	63	88.7	71	63	88.7	—	—	—
Los Angeles	80	66	82.5	80	66	82.5	—	—	—
Birmingham	15	6	40.0	14	5	35.7	1	1	100.0
Total	1,247	755	60.5	888	553	62.3	359	202	56.3

Source: U.S. Post Office Department.

[a] Winston-Salem and Charlotte SMSA's, that were included in the sample used elsewhere in this study, have been excluded from this analysis because the Post Office Department does not employ tractor trailer or motor vehicle operators in these two SMSA's.

[b] The figures under this heading also include substitute employees.

[c] Denver fills these positions as necessary.

ployers. At the same time, however, 87 percent of the companies interviewed who did employ Negroes maintained that they were excellent workers, or that as a group their dependability was no worse than that of the average white employee performing the same task.

It might be argued that the federal government is fostering racial job equality at any price, or that the lack of urgency prevailing throughout the bureaucratic structure of the Post Office Department is the type of work setting in which poorly motivated Negroes can perform best. These objections could, of course, be true to a degree, but the difference in the percentage of Negroes employed by the Department and the ratio found in private industry is just too great—63.7 percent versus 2.7 percent—to justify such objections. Several Department supervisors even informed the author that white drivers from private carriers often cannot maneuver their equipment in and around Department platforms without assistance from their own drivers, including the Negro ones. In brief, there is no substantial evidence whatsoever in support of the contention that Negro drivers employed by this federal agency are incompetent.

Tractor trailer drivers employed by the POD are included in the Post Office Field Service Classification No. 7. Depending upon their seniority, these drivers earn from $6,044 to $8,266 per year. Although on a national basis in 1967 18.9 percent of all postal employees were Negroes,[44] only 8.1 percent of all employees in PFS level No. 7 were Negroes. The percentage of Negroes employed as road drivers (63.7) is thus far above both the percentage of Negro employees for the Post Office Department as a whole and PFS No. 7 in particular. The differences found in the data above are sufficient to counter the employers' suggestion that Negroes are employed for social and political reasons rather than for their qualifications.

Three Negro drivers questioned at the Philadelphia Post Office recounted how, in 1962, they tried to obtain road jobs with a private carrier, whose name they mentioned. They stated that they were denied employment because the Teamsters and the employer gave them the "run around." This consisted of their continually being told that they lacked the proper training. As of 1966, this same firm had no Negroes in any of its job classifications. It is interesting to note that the Post Office Department

---

44. These data come from an in-house survey conducted by the Post Office Department in 1967.

supervisors claim that a person who can drive smaller trucks can be trained (in an 80-hour course which they sponsor) to handle the more cumbersome tractor trailers.

The "Loss of Customers" Argument

Employers are sometimes apprehensive about hiring Negroes for the first time because they fear this would occasion the loss of customers. In recent years it has become less of a problem because white consumers are becoming used to seeing Negroes in a greater variety of jobs.[45]

With the exception of two contract carriers, none of the other 111 firms interviewed thought customer reaction had any bearing on why they employed so few Negroes. Even the two firms that expressed a fear of losing business if they hired Negroes were somewhat vague as to why shippers would turn to other carriers, but they implied that some people believe that a firm that employs a disproportionate number of Negroes is second-rate. Contract carriers are different from the common carriers in that they serve a few select customers; thus, the firm's racial employment profile is easy for the customers to detect. Ironically, contract carriers who worry about customer reaction employ proportionately more Negroes than the common carriers who maintain that the possible loss of customers does not influence their hiring of Negroes.

The consensus among most companies was that their drivers seldom come in direct contact with the shippers but rather with other drivers, platform men, and helpers. Consequently, it is unlikely that the apprehension over a general customer revolt contributes to the industry's reaction to equal employment programs. It might be well to note that among private carriers where drivers are often salesmen, the reaction of the consumer was a factor in establishing hiring policies.[46]

---

45. Georges F. Doriot (supervisor), *The Management of Racial Integration in Business*, Special Report to Management, Harvard Graduate School of Business Administration (New York: McGraw-Hill, 1964), p. 82; see also, Edward C. Koziara and Karen S. Koziara, *The Negro in the Hotel Industry*, The Racial Policies of American Industry, Report No. 4 (Philadelphia: Industrial Research Unit, The Wharton School of Finance and Commerce, University of Pennsylvania, 1968), p. 35.

46. New York State Commission Against Discrimination, *The Employment of Negroes as Driver Salesmen in the Baking Industry* (New York: The Commission, 1960).

The Reaction of White Employees

Presumably, many industries would label a white rank and file revolt caused by the employment of Negroes as a sociological and psychological difficulty rather than as an economic issue. Through coercion and persuasion, supervisors in some self-contained work settings have been able to discipline white employees reacting adversely to the hiring of Negroes. Because of the special nature of the trucking industry, however, there can be some unusual economic consequences if fleetmen insist upon hiring Negroes against the will of the white majority. Once the vehicle leaves the terminal, supervisory personnel have no direct control over the activities of the driver. Private studies have been conducted for the industry to determine the approximate amount of time various long haul and even city runs should take. Spotters often are hired by the larger companies to check on their road drivers, and drivers are notified if they exceed the posted speed limits or if they are guilty of other safety violations. In this loosely disciplined work setting, companies hiring Negroes might face a rebellious rank and file which would give vent to their displeasure not by *violating* speed and safety regulations, but rather by *observing* them. This is particularly true in local or city operations. For should a driver choose to observe all the motor vehicle regulations in any given city, the movement of goods could well slow down to such a degree that shippers would start turning to another motor carrier, or purchase their own fleet of trucks and become one among the many private carriers.

Although employers are aware of their responsibility to have their drivers observe safety regulations, they sometimes take the risk of dispatching trailers whose weights exceed the maximum prescribed by law. They are not unaware that drivers double park in congested downtown city streets, carry excess weight loads over bridges, and violate the posted speed limits. The subtle sabotage on the part of white drivers of following all the rules would leave the employer with no recourse before the law or the Teamsters. Of all the economic consequences arising because an employer hired Negroes, this could be the most costly and the most difficult to control.

Teamster members realize that legal slowdowns of this nature may cost a carrier customers, and ultimately may force it out of business. Generally, however, the attitude of the rank and file is that the demand for motor carrier service is unlimited, and they are willing to follow the freight as it goes from one carrier to another. Since drivers work alone for a greater part of the day, they have a tendency to identify more with the union and job opportunities at large than with a particular firm. Employers and union personnel alike acknowledge that this is a formidable obstacle to the creation of effective fair employment practices.

One employer aptly stated:

I might hire a few Negro road drivers if I could find some that I was convinced would be reliable and handle my equipment safely and courteously. But I'm not ready to risk absenteeism, damaged equipment, fights, slowdowns, or other problems with my present drivers. Besides, I've got a good crew here; we get along, you know what I mean, and why bust all that up? Anyhow no damn government can tell me how to run my business.[47]

Approaches to Recruitment

Because the private carriers have grown in such a topsy-turvy fashion, and since their hiring procedures have been subjected to extraordinary pressures exerted by the Teamsters, their screening and hiring procedures are riddled with fetishes and contradictions. Needless to say, the industry is of the opinion that their hiring techniques are reasonable and uniformly administered. Its sole justification for this claim seems to be that it obtains employees when needed. Some firms in hiring road drivers, for example, will not hire anyone with too high an I.Q., claiming that intelligent people daydream as they drive and that they have a tendency to be trouble makers, often meaning potential union leaders. Simultaneously, other companies welcome intelligent applicants for road driving postitions because they believe that they make better drivers. It is not unusual to find two nearly identical firms bidding for long haul drivers in the same labor market, but setting different age and experience standards for new applicants. For example, while one firm insists on having its new road drivers undergo its own formal driver training programs and will not permit local drivers to become road drivers and vice versa, another firm possessing identical corporate characteristics will insist that all road drivers must have worked with them as local drivers. Last, but not least, the total person must be judged before allowing him full responsibility over the company's equipment. Obviously, where unproven, nebulous, and inconsistent hiring procedures prevail, it is easy to judge Negroes

---

47. "Trucking Comes Under the Civil Rights Gun," *Commercial Car Journal* (June 1966), p. 108.

as totally different persons who are not to be trusted on their own. Moreover, when the government puts pressure on the companies to hire Negro road drivers, they immediately point to their highest standards for admission, when it is evident that these standards are relaxed when whites apply for employment.

There is some merit in the position that personnel directors should establish policies compelling terminal managers to hire the best applicants. Industry leaders report, however, that except for those of five or six of the larger carriers, personnel staffs are not necessarily qualified to select the best. Many personnel people have been taken out of drivers' ranks and few have had formal training in personnel relations; often they attend seminars in highway safety, and, in some instances, the safety directors serve as personnel directors. Part of the problem causing diverse hiring standards to prevail is the lack of qualified leadership. This leadership vacuum is of even greater significance as the government prods the industry to view Negro employment in terms of affirmative action programs. Better managed firms, which are usually the larger ones, issue employment manuals to their terminal managers. These manuals spell out the Department of Transportation's and the firm's qualifications for each job specification and the procedures to be followed in interviewing, screening, and testing applicants. Terminal or operations managers make the initial hiring decision at the local level. Because of the geographical distribution of the terminals, headquarters screens the hiring of road drivers by checking out the veracity of the information submitted by the new employee.

Smaller firms frequently bypass the screening process in the hiring of drivers. Representatives of the union find themselves confronted with cases during grievance hearings in which they are compelled to represent the interests of a man whom the firm never should have hired in the first place. Employers concede that in such cases the union usually is extremely fair. Should a local union be going through the throes of an internal political feud, however, this same driver may become a *cause celebre* for one of the feuding factions. In this case, the floating incompetent driver can be extremely costly to the company.

One of the most difficult procedures to police in the hiring of drivers is the road test, in which the applicant actually drives a truck in the company of one of the senior drivers. It is common in smaller firms for a driving applicant to find that the screening process consists of nothing but a road test. The one responsible for hiring will simply say to one of the senior drivers, "See if this guy can drive." The applicant is then taken to whatever place the senior driver selects for a road test. If the applicant is a Negro, there is no way for the company to evaluate the degree to which a senior driver's possible anti-Negro biases may influence his evaluation of the man.

Some Teamster locals are more powerful than others. It is not unusual, moreover, to find that companies party to the same contract are treated differently by a local. The unevenness of local union strength and the special privileges enjoyed by some companies permit certain employers to bypass contract provisions. Where local unions are aggressive and constantly questioning any change in the companies' operations, the latter have a tendency to abide scrupulously by terms specified in the contract. Besides providing for a union shop, the National Freight Agreement also states:

When the employer needs additional men he shall give the Local Union equal opportunity with all other sources to provide suitable applicants, but the Employer shall not be required to hire those referred by the Local Union.[48]

Here, the company clearly has the final say over hiring employees, yet some employers point to this clause in explaining the absence of Negroes. It is probably true, however, that some employers, having been harrassed and unrelentingly badgered by the IBT, usually ask the shop steward or business agent if any union member is looking for employment. Of greater significance than the terms of the contract, in regard to Negro employment, is the fact that employers rely mainly on an informal referral method in the hiring of dockmen, helpers, and mechanics, as well as drivers.

Companies constituting the sample of this study were questioned as to what sources they found best in recruiting hourly employees (Table 13). They were asked to rank these choices according to the order of their importance. At first glance it is easy to see that employers as a rule do not rely on either newspaper ads or employment agencies. Manpower needs are essentially met by employers first asking present employees if they know of anyone seeking employment, and second, by going to the IBT. The other source noted by employers consists of

---

48. National Master Freight Agreement, Article 3, Section I(c).

TABLE 13. *Trucking Industry*
Employers' Preference as to Sources of
Recruitment of Hourly Employees

Sources	1st Choice	2nd Choice	3rd Choice	4th Choice	5th Choice
Newspaper ads	—	2	1	—	3
The union	32	41	13	7	—
Referrals	62	43	30	12	—
Employment agencies	—	—	3	—	1
Others	2	10	47	53	13

Source: Personal interviews.

Note: Some employers were so vague about the sources they used to obtain new hires that they were not included; nevertheless, over 90 percent of all respondents are included.

pirating employees from other trucking companies or absorbing the employees of a company which has moved its terminal facilities or merged with another carrier. United Parcel Service in Philadelphia, for example, was involved in a protracted labor dispute in 1967, resulting in the facility being permanently closed down. It is estimated that 800 competent drivers, dockmen, and mechanics (only a few of whom were Negroes) were thrown into the Philadelphia labor market. Both informal referrals and union contracts expose the companies to a very narrow slice of all labor markets. This fact must be weighed against the companies' contention that experienced Negro employees are not available.

Indeed, where firms employ only one or two Negroes or none at all, there is little likelihood that Negro applicants will be forthcoming. As job openings arise, terminal managers will ask their employees if they know anyone looking for a job and within a racially segregated society white employees will rarely refer Negroes. Clusters of friends, relatives, neighbors, or schoolmates dominate in some terminals. Like other blue collar workers, employees view job opportunities as conquered small kingdoms over which they have the right to divide the spoils.

Responses to a question as to how long Negroes have been employed corroborated the results obtained regarding sources of employment. The longer that firms had employed Negroes, the higher the percentage of Negro employees.

The Teamsters' Union as a source for new hires can function in two ways: (1) terminal supervisory personnel can ask the steward or business agent if any of "his boys" are interested in permanent work, or (2) employers can call the IBT's hiring hall for casual drivers. Union officials constitute an informal information system on the availability of drivers, platform men, and mechanics. Disgruntled union members keep the business agents informed of their wanting to change jobs. Business agents also are aware of changes in companies' operations and of mergers. Anti-Negro sentiment and the political constraints within a local militate against union officials recommending Negro union members for the more desirable jobs. Some terminals, labeled "Negro barns" by union members, are sent only Negro washers, oilers, helpers, and dockmen. In an industry where there are relatively few Negroes in the first place, it is highly unlikely that many Negroes will be found in the ever-fluid and more desirable driver pool.

Except in the South, the Teamsters maintain hiring halls in the larger cities having a concentration of terminals. Should an employer need a temporary driver (referred to as a casual driver), he will telephone the hall and make his needs known. The employers constantly complain about these floaters, who, they contend, are poor drivers, more interested in playing checkers and enjoying companionship at the hall than they are in working. Despite such complaints, the industry objected vehemently when the IBT tried to close some of its halls, and they were reopened. Carriers often need extra local drivers before Christmas, when merchandisers are stocking their shelves, and on Mondays and Fridays during the year because neither they nor the shippers want the shipments standing still over the weekends. Halls, therefore, provide the employers with a necessary and flexible manpower pool. If the relationship between the company and the union has been somewhat amiable, the employer is given the opportunity to choose from the available drivers. Companies, however, often maintain a list of the better floating drivers, so that if a permanent opening occurs, they will specify a particular man.

When Negro drivers "bat out of the hall," they are often sent out on dirty and difficult jobs. If Negroes are sent out to the better paying and easier jobs, they mysteriously do not seem to remain with one of these employers long enough to gain seniority rights. Some employers insist that they have been calling the hall for years, and they have never been sent a single Negro. Inasmuch as Negro casuals without seniority rights save the employer money—and because local union leaders do not want a white rebellion on their hands—it is advantageous to both parties surreptitiously to exclude Negroes from permanent employment.

Seniority Provisions

Although the National Master Freight Agreement embodies guidelines relating to seniority provisions, the numerous regional and local supplemental agreements contain certain exceptions and amendments. In the event that two companies merge or consolidate, the National Agreement provides that the IBT and the acquiring firm must mutually agree on how the once separate seniority lists are to be blended. Besides this broad statement of mutual agreement the contract also contains specific rules and regulations that are to be followed.

In an industry where mergers, acquisitions, and consolidations are common, these rules governing seniority are necessary. Mergers usually are followed by a total revamping of the carriers' operations and the shutdown of certain terminals. No doubt some employees are affected adversely in these corporate and operational changes, but there is no evidence that the Teamsters or the companies purposely agree to changes in seniority rosters to lay off Negroes. Other seniority provisions, however, may militate against hiring Negroes, and also may inhibit the Negroes' mobility in the job hierarchy.

The National Master Freight Agreement states, "The extent to which seniority shall be applied as well as the methods and procedures of such application shall be set forth in each of the Supplemental Agreements." [49] This broad mandate gives rise to an infinite variety of seniority provisions throughout the country.

---

49. National Master Freight Agreement, Article 5, Section I.

The general rule is that drivers can bid[50] on various runs and those at the top of the list bid first. To familiarize the drivers with the options open to them, the employer must post the runs in a conspicuous place. Since some hauls pay more, and because some necessitate that drivers remain away from home for longer durations of time, senior drivers are given the first choice at what they subjectively consider to be the best run.

Open bidding could adversely affect Negro employment in two ways. First, as a general rule white drivers resent Negroes who have more seniority than they do and open bidding constantly reminds the white driver that a Negro is earning more than he is for the same kind of work. Second, as the bidding progresses down the seniority list, some runs are bypassed and the employer must make the assignment himself. He may be compelled, for reasons of economy, to assign a white and Negro together in a sleeper-cab operation. For obvious reasons, companies are apprehensive about such an arrangement and argue that they lose a needed flexibility in assigning drivers by having Negroes among them.

Any employer who compels a white driver to ride with a Negro in a sleeper cab must be willing to face the clandestine sabotage that the white rank and file can shower upon him. Feigned grievances, which will be discussed later, may start cropping up all over. Nevertheless, in one case in which an employer categorically told a white driver that if he refused to ride with an assigned Negro driver, he would be discharged, the white driver reluctantly accepted the assignment, and the employer was faced with neither grievances nor slowdowns. This exceptional case is no doubt explained by the fact that the company was one of the giants of the industry, and had taken a firm stand against discrimination. By way of contrast, another large carrier allegedly promised its white employees that regardless of what the government says or does, it will never hire Negro road drivers.

---

50. The Supplemental Agreement for Local 85 in San Francisco reads: "Job seniority will be used in bidding for assignments to equipment. . . ." Section 7. The Supplemental Agreement covering seven IBT locals in Philadelphia and vicinity states: "All regular runs (except those 'House Concerns' with original drivers), positions, starting time, classification and shifts are subject to seniority and shall be posted for bids. Posting shall be at a conspicuous place so that all eligible employees will receive notice of the vacancy, run or position open for bid, and such posting of bids shall be made not more than once each calendar year; vacancies, new runs, new positions shall be posted for bid immediately, unless otherwise mutually agreed upon. Peddle runs shall be subject to bidding provided driver is qualified." Section 4(a).

Carriers with road drivers, local drivers, and dockmen working out of the same terminal may have a single seniority list or several of them. If an employee switches from the local drivers' list to the road seniority roster, he must go to the bottom of the latter. If an employer has an opening among his road drivers, he usually will give the men at the top of the local list the opportunity to fill this job opening. Purely subjective reasons influence the local drivers' decision to accept or reject this offer. Although there are no reliable data on the subject, it is estimated that once a man has ten or more years seniority on the local roster, he is reluctant to risk his seniority rights by switching to long haul driving. With a greater percentage of Negroes employed as local drivers, it would seem that many of them could gain entry into the firm through this door, and then be promoted to the better-paying, long haul work, but such is not the case. Carriers maintaining both local and road seniority lists contend that Negroes themselves refuse these better jobs. Yet, the same carriers agree that white drivers are willing to accept the risk and move from the top of a local seniority roster to the bottom of a road list. Since the employer must determine competency for road work, he is not forced to use seniority alone in making these promotions. At the same time, the Negro is starkly aware of the economic pressures exerted upon the employer and the sociological adjustments he must make within the various work groups. Although seniority is not a bottleneck to whites on the promotional ladder, it often is an obstacle for Negroes because of the personal risks involved.

Grievance Procedures

In most industries unions and management alike run the risk of having discrimination charges lodged against them in the event an arbitration decision is handed down against a Negro employee, even if the Negro is deserving of an adverse decision. When a Negro is party to a case submitted to arbitration, those responsible for deciding the case take the possible charge of discrimination into account. In most grievance procedures the onus of proving nondiscrimination is shared by an impartial arbitrator. The Teamsters, however, have fashioned what is known as an open-end grievance procedure which seldom permits the use of an impartial arbitrator and gives the union a leverage technique which most employers fear. This "major control mechanism" [51] allows for the union to call a strike if both sides fail to reach agreement in a given case. According to James:

> . . . in a collective bargaining structure which stresses uniformity, the open-end grievance procedure, operating without precedent, enables the union to behave, to a degree at least, like a discriminating monopolist. The contract may be enforced more stringently against employers who can afford to provide better conditions while it retains the advantages derived from apparent equality.[52]

Inasmuch as neither side in a dispute in the trucking industry is hampered by precedent, there is a tendency to trade grievances off. The trucking industry cannot stockpile the services it sells, and "in the absence of fixed rules and standards, the union invariably wields the upper hand at grievance meetings, for strikes are dreaded by most trucking operators." [53] This does not imply that the Teamsters always hold trump cards over every employer. A decision in a given grievance case, however, may well become the basis of a union demand at the next collective bargaining session. So employers must weigh a single case in terms of future costs.

In an arbitrary grievance setting, where grievances are more readily traded off at lower levels, no employer wants unnecessary complaints to arise simply because he insisted upon the hiring of Negroes. The shop steward or the business agent, depending on who handles grievances, could insist upon a literal interpretation of the contract and thus constrain the employer in his day-to-day operations. If the employer fails to comply precisely with specific terms of the contract, grievances might well be cropping up every time he made a decision. To the degree an employer has won special concessions from the IBT, either in grievance cases or in changes of his operations, to the same degree he owes something to the union officials who granted the favors. One of the concessions the employer might make in return is his guarantee not to employ Negroes—especially if pressure from the rank and file is being put on the union official himself. In brief, employers view the hiring of Negroes against the will of the rank and file as "muddying the water" in a situation where their problems with, and the reaction of, the Teamsters is unpredictable and potentially costly.

---

51. James, *op. cit.*, p. 168.

52. *Ibid.*, p. 172.

53. *Ibid.*, p. 171.

The Availability of Public Accommodations

Another variable, noted in Chapter III, which militated against the hiring of Negro road drivers in the South was their inability to find eating and sleeping facilities prior to the enactment of federal legislation outlawing discrimination in public accommodations. Fearing that the hiring of Negroes would lead to a certain inflexibility in assigning drivers, the employers singled out the public accommodations problem as a reason for not hiring Negro road drivers. In turn, this facilitated the creation of all-white, tightly-knit work groups, characterized by considerable cohesiveness. Although the enactment of federal legislation now outlaws such discrimination, Negroes are still excluded from the white fraternity.

Larger carriers maintain their own dormitories located in or near the strategic breaking-point terminals. Although this enables the company to operate more sleeper cab vehicles, the Teamsters contend it also has a tendency to keep men away from home too long. Interestingly enough in several instances where companies have hired Negro road drivers and white drivers have been compelled to accept them in the dormitories there have been no problems. One southern firm commented on the fact that in one of their dormitories which previously had been all white, the Negro drivers had been seen playing checkers with white employees. Most carriers, however, remain reluctant to assign runs to Negroes if the run requires them to sleep in company dormitories.

A carrier domiciled in the South hired two Negro road drivers for a sleeper cab run. Both of these drivers proved to be relatively competent, but after about six months one of them quit. Ostensibly, he left this carrier because his wife was against his being away from home several nights a week. But, in fact, the attitude of the white drivers also influenced his decision to seek employment as a local driver elsewhere.[54]

Nearness to Negro Labor Markets

The final variable helping to explain Negro employment patterns in the various labor markets is that most terminals are not located near the sections of cities where Negroes are concentrated. The author can attest to this because, as he visited

54. Personal interview, 1968.

the many and varied cities throughout the country, he discovered that the wharves of San Francisco, narrow streets under the Brooklyn Bridge, and unpaved cinder roads in the South were not accessible to public transportation. The older terminals, once located in what are now urban ghetto neighborhoods, have been moved closer to the industrial parks orbiting the nation's cities. Some carriers moved from the hub cities to avoid congested traffic patterns. Also, as the inner city neighborhoods started to disintegrate, carriers moved to avoid pilferage and damage to their properties and equipment. Although the majority of firms moved prior to the beginning of the racial unrest that has recently plagued our cities, the effect is that the trucking industry is no longer within easy access for Negro labor.

As an interesting illustration of this factor in Negro employment a company representative in Philadelphia noted that his company had several Negro local drivers who had been working for the carrier for over twenty years and were now at the top of the seniority list. Yet there was a long gap between those found at the top of the seniority list and three new Negro employees found at the bottom of the seniority list. A tight wartime labor market situation may have accounted for the firm hiring these few Negroes over twenty years ago, but the employer attributed these hirings to the fact that the terminal had been located near a Negro neighborhood, but moved away eighteen years ago. He also said that the older Negro drivers "having arrived" were reluctant to recommend either friends or relatives when job openings were available. The new Negro employees had come in off of the street when drivers were in short supply. The employer believed that they had applied because lately Negroes have acquired enough courage to seek employment outside of their "known world." Therefore, to the degree that distance in the absence of adequate public transportation constitutes a barrier to the mobility of Negroes in the nation's labor markets, it is valid to assume that this factor partially explains the relatively low ratio of Negroes found in the industry.

LOCAL DRIVERS AND HELPERS

Hiring standards for local drivers are not quite as stringent as those for road drivers. The nature of these two different driving jobs has influenced the employer's use of a different set of criteria to determine competency. Unlike the long-haul driver, who spends practically all of his time driving a large tractor trailer, the local driver spends considerable time in loading and unloading freight transported in smaller vehicles. Sometimes these "peddle" drivers,[55] as they are called, have a helper who does not drive, but helps the driver load and unload the freight. The Teamsters, over the years, have permitted employers to use fewer helpers if they passed some of the savings in wages on to the local drivers; helpers are consequently disappearing from the scene. Because the local cartage agreements are supplemental agreements appended to the national freight agreement, the wage rates and provisions permitting the use of helpers vary from area to area.

Since most of the local operations take place in urban or suburban areas where freight is moved from terminals, warehouses, and factories to wholesalers and retailers, local drivers are more likely to come in contact with consumers than are road drivers, and terminal managers take this into account in hiring. Those wishing to become local drivers must be familiar with the layout of a city, the location of specific streets, and local parking regulations. Such requirements work against many urban Negroes who, even if they are not new arrivals in a city, may not have had the necessary experience to meet these requirements.

Our 1968 sample found that 10.9 percent of all local drivers were Negroes. It would seem that the normal line of progression from local to road driver should afford Negroes the opportunity to gain admission to the better-paying road jobs, but for reasons discussed in a previous section of this chapter, this is not the case. Some of the employers generally interested in promoting equal employment have indicated that in the last few years they have made a concerted effort to hire Negroes as local drivers in those terminals employing the least number of Negroes. Hopefully, the Negroes' presence could dilute the deep anti-Negro prejudices held by predominantly white work crews,

---

55. The Ohio Rider to the Central States area over-the-road Motor Freight Supplemental Agreement states:

> A Local or Peddle-Run Driver shall be one who originates and terminates at his Domicile Terminal daily and whose duties are pick-up and delivery service only from or to consignee or shipper. However, a Peddle or Local Run that is now established as such by the Employer shall not be disturbed unless proven to the satisfaction of the Committee representing the Union and the Employer's Group, that the same is subterfuge to defeat the purpose of this Agreement.

and induce more Negroes to apply and more employers to accept them for long haul driving jobs.

NONDRIVER MANUAL WORKERS

Trucks usually are loaded during the evening by dockmen or, as they are sometimes called, platform men. These jobs can be filled by any male able to read bills of lading and physically capable of handling the freight passing through the firm's terminal location. Most dockmen earn less than the local drivers but more than the helpers. If they work on the dock as fork-lift operators—and not as platform men per se—their hourly rate of pay is often the same as that paid to local drivers.

The percentage of platform men and fork-lift operators employed at any given terminal location, in relationship to the total number of employees, depends on whether or not the type of freight handled permits palletization. Unlike those applying for driver jobs, applicants for dock positions do not find safety and health regulations a hurdle to entry. In these less prestigious jobs Negroes have found employment much easier to obtain. In 1968, our sample showed that 12.7 percent of all dockmen were Negroes.

Transportation equipment is the one single item for which trucking firms must allocate most of their capital. If they are to protect their investment in moving stock, and if they intend to keep the shipping public satisfied by avoiding breakdowns on the road, they must sponsor comprehensive preventive maintenance programs. Mechanics, tiremen, greasers, and washers are responsible for keeping the company's equipment in excellent operating condition. The titles indicate the job content, but it is not unusual to find an employee with the title of mechanic greasing the trucks and changing tires.

The type of work performed, in conjunction with seniority, determines whether or not a mechanic should be considered a journeyman mechanic, the highest formal classification a mechanic can achieve, which pays the highest union wage rate.[56] In turn, it is not unusual for the top mechanic of a particular shop to receive wages in excess of what is specified in the contract.

---

56. Most shop personnel belong to the International Association of Machinists AFL-CIO. In some areas the Teamsters include these employees in their local unions.

The nonspecialist employed at the terminal level may be hired as a "jack of all trades" and classified as a helper. With truck manufacturers extending the warranty period, the firms are hiring more of what they call "part replacers." Employees engaged as full-time washers, tire changers, and lubricators, or who perform a combination of these jobs, are at the bottom of the job scale and classified as miscellaneous garage employees. There are so many intra- and inter-firm variations regarding the classification and pay differentials of garage personnel that pay scales spelled out in contracts are not necessarily indicative of the hourly rate. Nevertheless, journeymen mechanics make in the area of $4.00 per hour, and in union shops those at the bottom of the pay scale usually make a dollar or more less. Negroes are commonly employed as helpers.

MANAGEMENT PERSONNEL

Except for top executives, management in the trucking industry is relatively low paid.[57] It is conceded generally by personnel directors that low starting salaries, coupled with an apparently unchallenging future, deter college graduates from entering the industry. As a general rule, the degree to which management positions are competently filled is in direct proportion to the size of the firm. The smaller firms usually rely on family members to fill decision-making positions, and it is not unusual to find management personnel who started out as truck drivers or terminal managers. Yet this tradition of coming up through the ranks is slowly dying out as the number of smaller firms declines.

Successful, highly profitable firms have grown so fast that in many cases they have not given enough attention to the recruitment of management personnel. Some have attempted to compensate for these shortcomings by inaugurating their own management training programs. College graduates are being recruit-

---

57. For a more detailed account of some of the problems discussed in this chapter, see the Proceedings of the Annual National Forum on Trucking Industrial Relations. These publications are as follows: 11th Annual National Forum, *Organizing Trucking Management* (1959) ; 12th Annual National Forum, *Personnel Practices in the Trucking Industry* (1961) ; 13th Annual National Forum, *Motivating Middle Management in Trucking* (1962) ; 15th Forum, *Profit Sharing and Incentives for Trucking Employees* (1965) (Washington: American Trucking Associations, Inc.).

ed as salesmen, maintenance engineers, terminal managers, accountants, personnel specialists, and safety directors. Although the above list is not exhaustive, it is representative of the various job opportunities available to a college graduate with a degree in transportation, marketing, or general business.

The number of Negroes in these training programs is small but growing. Competition for trained black graduates is great, however, and trucking companies are not bidding heavily in this market. With only 0.1 percent of its management personnel Negro in 1968, the trucking industry must undertake a concerted program if more Negroes are to be employed as managers. The problem of equal employment opportunities at this level of the job hierarchy is somewhat reflective of the industry's inability to establish comprehensive management training programs for blacks and whites alike. Since Negroes have not been able to bring economic pressure to bear upon the industry, and since, further, the great majority of firms are family controlled, the idea of having Negroes as managers is something that trucking management did not seriously consider prior to 1965.

Middle Management

Each terminal employing approximately 200 persons requires a variety of administrative positions. The terminal manager is responsible to the home office for the total operations of the terminal, including the hiring and dismissal of employees. To assist him there also may be an operations manager who directs the work on the platform, and an office manager who is in charge of the clerical force. Most of the present terminal, operations, and office managers have come up through the ranks. Inasmuch as there were few Negro drivers hired over the years, there are now even fewer in these managerial positions today.

Large firms have regional supervisors who serve as intermediaries between headquarters and the numerous terminal managers. They may have as many as twenty terminals under their jurisdiction. Again, the larger and better-managed firms are replacing supervisory personnel who came up through the ranks with younger men from their management training programs.

The salary of the terminal manager, which is much higher than that of an operations or office manager, may range from $10,000 to $14,000 per year. Most firms determine terminal managers' salaries by the terminal's revenue and annual profits. Nevertheless, many terminal managers make less than the senior drivers. In any case, employers are still reluctant to have Negroes coordinate the work of predominantly all-white work crews.

Dispatchers

The dispatcher's primary function is to coordinate and plan the movement of freight between terminals. He telephones the drivers to let them know when they are needed, assigns loads, and works closely with the garage to obtain various types of equipment. The dispatcher must be familiar with the geographical area covered by the system, labor contracts and the most recent interpretations of these contracts, and Interstate Commerce Commission regulations. He must be able to provide the drivers with directions in the event of a breakdown, accident, or any other unforeseen delay while out on the road. In brief, it is the dispatcher's duty to see that the company's equipment and manpower are used in the most economical and profitable manner, consonant with efficient service for the customer.

Like other supervisory personnel employed by the majority of firms at the terminal level, most dispatchers have previously been drivers. After spending years behind the wheel of a large tractor trailer or fighting city traffic on local runs, drivers sometimes welcome the responsibility and prestige associated with the dispatcher's job. Some drivers, however, refuse dispatching responsibilities because they often can earn more driving a truck. Again, the method of selecting dispatchers and the fact that the crews supervised are almost all white militates against Negroes occupying these jobs. In 1968, only 0.2 percent of all dispatchers employed by the sample firms were Negroes.

CLERICAL WORKERS

In addition to female typists and file clerks, other clerical jobs in trucking, sometimes staffed by men, include rate clerks, manifest clerks, cashiers, tracing clerks, and O.S.D. (over freight, short, and damage) clerks. At small terminal locations, women secretaries usually perform a variety of clerical jobs. The larger terminals will have a number of clerks, depending on the volume of traffic handled.

The most demanding job is that of the rate clerk, who must be thoroughly familiar with a host of prevailing rates for a vast number of commodities hauled. Billing clerks, the most numerous of all the clerical workers, transfer information from the bill of lading to the freight bill which is subsequently sent to the shipper. They must be fast and accurate typists, and earned approximately $2.75 per hour in 1968. Billing clerks are a class all to themselves and have a tendency to float from firm to firm, apparently feeling that the job will somehow become more challenging if they do not remain at any one terminal for too long. Many of the billing clerks employed by the industry started out as file clerks with a pay scale ranging from $1.60 to $1.85 an hour.

In 1968, 3.0 percent of the male clerical workers and 2.3 percent of the female clerical help were Negroes. In the small firms there were no Negro clerical employees. Smaller firms have so few employees doing clerical work that a "sorority" type of attitude prevails and Negroes are not welcome. Although the larger carriers admit that this is relatively an easier area in which to pursue equal employment, they must bid against other industries, whose offices are more accessible to public transportation and who can often offer female Negro applicants higher salaries and better working conditions.

Of all the jobs available in the trucking industry, sampled firms found the various clerical jobs usually performed by men (rate clerks, billing clerks, manifest clerks, and O.S.D. clerks) usually the most difficult to fill. In some areas of the country, special training programs have been established to meet the need for an adequate supply of competent clerks. Employers seem more willing to hire Negro male clerks than they have been to employ Negroes as road drivers and in management positions. This willingness is probably attributable to the tight labor market conditions.

THE IBT AND CIVIL RIGHTS

We have already noted in the previous chapter that civil rights was not high on the Teamsters agenda under President James R. Hoffa, or under his predecessors. The IBT attitude is illustrated further by action to a resolution introduced at the 1966 IBT National Convention by a Negro delegate from a Los Angeles freight drivers' union. It read in part:

NOW THEREFORE BE IT RESOLVED, that this International Union expresses its endorsement and extends its united support in furtherance of removing each and every barrier and injustice which is inherent within the deadly seeds of racial discrimination and prejudice.

BE IT FURTHER RESOLVED, that the facilities of this International Union shall be available in support of any and every program which may be determined by the General President of this Union, designed to give meaning and intent to the carrying out of this resolution.[58]

Vice President Harold Gibbons, who had been executive assistant to Hoffa until December 1963, commented that the Teamsters adhered to a policy of nondiscrimination stressed by Hoffa when he assumed office in 1958. Consequently, the Teamsters eliminated those "few examples of Jim Crow local unions which existed around the country." [59] Gibbons also mentioned that the General Executive Board had passed a resolution in support of the whole Negro community.

More significant than Gibbons' broad observations about the Teamsters' nondiscrimination policy was his admission that two local unions rebelled when the International gave $25,000 to the late Dr. Martin Luther King, Jr.[60] The anti-Negro sentiment in these locals was so strong that Hoffa had to speak personally to the membership of one of the locals, while Gibbons spoke to the other.

The only applause during Gibbons' speech came when he tied the plight of the Negro with the necessity of voting antiunion Congressmen out of office. One attendant told the author that the applause at the end of the speech was cordial, but certainly not enthusiastic.[61]

With the conviction and jailing of Hoffa, the acting president, Frank Fitzsimmons, restored considerable local and regional autonomy. Given the background already described, there is no reason to suppose that this move will promote a more progressive Teamster attitude toward the employment of Negro long haul drivers.

The formation of the Alliance for Labor Action (ALA) by the Teamsters and the United Automobile, Aerospace and Agricultural Workers (UAW) in 1968 with a program stressing community action, drives to organize the unorganized, and civil rights is also not likely to alter the Teamster approach to Negro

---

58. International Brotherhood of Teamsters, Chauffeurs, Warehousemen and Helpers of America, *Proceedings—Nineteenth Convention* (Miami, Florida, July 4-7, 1966), p. 165.

59. *Ibid.*, p. 166.

60. *Ibid.*, p. 167.

61. Personal interview, 1968.

employment. In a number of areas, especially on the West Coast, Teamster locals and joint councils [62] have made grants to local poverty or community action groups, and otherwise acted "socially minded." [63] This, however, has not opened driver jobs to Negroes any more than Teamster organization on a nondiscriminatory basis in areas outside of motor transportation—which has occurred for many years—has altered its exclusivist approach to trucking. As we shall note in a later chapter, discrimination in the trucking industry has resulted in a number of law suits pursuant of Title VII of the Civil Rights Act, including charges of patterns of discrimination filed by the U.S. Department of Justice, which include both companies and the IBT as defendants. The facts alleged in these suits seem to indicate a continuation of past practices that do not seem to be affected by any new "socially-minded" approaches or goals.

The Alliance for Labor Action selected Atlanta as the location for its initial concerted campaign to organize an estimated 50,000 workers employed by companies located in the area of this southern industrial hub. Although Negroes are employed by these concerns, the ALA faces a real dilemma. It must project the image of being truly impartial toward the hiring of Negroes by all industries, including trucking, in order to attract those unorganized companies where Negroes constitute a majority. And, at the same time, it must not seem too pro-Negro, as employers having a predominantly white work force might try to use this to dissuade their employees from voting for unionization. For example, a company in Selma, Alabama [64] conveyed the notion to its white employees that the IBT's contribution to Dr. King, noted above, was indicative of the Teamsters' pro-Negro stance. In this case, the National Labor Relations Board sup-

---

62. Within the structure of the Teamsters there are joint councils: fifty-five in the United States and six in Canada. As early as 1904 joint councils were established to give the specialized locals in a metropolitan area strength in their bargaining activities, and to assist in settling any jurisdictional disputes which might arise between the locals. The joint councils are found in the major cities or they may include a whole state where the IBT is relatively weak, such as Arkansas. Inasmuch as these bodies of affiliated locals are not that important regarding civil rights, further elaboration is unnecessary.

63. See, for example, *The International Teamster*, Vol. 66, No. 9 (September 1969), p. 13 and Vol. 66, No. 11 (November 1969), p. 11.

64. For details, see Bush Hog, Inc., 161 NLRB No. 1136 (1966), as reported in *Race Relations Law Review* 505 (1967).

ported the trial examiner's contention that this reference, in conjunction with threats to integrate the plant if the union won, constituted a violation of Section 8(a)(1) of the National Labor Relations Act. This company blatantly exploited the Negro problem in an effort to persuade its employees to reject overtures of the IBT, but others are learning to be more surreptitious in reference to the Negro issue, and thus avoid the censure of the NLRB.

There are, to be sure, significant personal consequences that might befall a local Teamster leader, especially in the South, should he take the lead or cooperate with trucking employers in the hiring or promoting of Negroes as over-the-road drivers. Unlike their national counterparts, local union officials must be more responsive to the aspirations and wishes of the rank and file. Thus, local union officials might be voted out of office should they fail to take into account that their constituents often harbor deep-seated anti-Negro sentiments.

CHAPTER V

Regional and City Differences, 1968

In this chapter we will use 1968 employment data to describe the patterns of Negro employment within four broad geographical regions and thirteen distinct Standard Metropolitan Statistical Areas. We shall find that the differences in Negro employment among regions and SMSA's are differences of degree, corroborating the findings in the previous chapter. The subsequent racial employment statistics reported on the basis of four distinct geographical areas, the Northeast, South, Midwest, and West, were derived by expanding the original data obtained through research in the field. (See Appendixes A and B for details.)

NEGRO EMPLOYMENT IN THE NORTHEAST

Data representative of ten SMSA's located in the Northeast region [65] of the country were derived from the three following sample SMSA's: Philadelphia, New York, and Boston. Company representatives from thirty-four firms with corporate headquarters in these three SMSA's were interviewed. Of this total, eleven were large firms, employing 101 or more, and twenty-three were small firms employing one hundred or less.

The percentage of Negroes employed in all job classifications for firms with corporate headquarters in forty-eight SMSA's throughout the country was 7.6, while the Northeast, as Table 14 shows, has a 9.8 percent Negro work force. When the three sample SMSA's in the Northeast are viewed independently, the percentage of Negroes employed in each is as follows: Philadelphia, 10.5 percent; New York, 15.8 percent; and Boston, 1.4 percent. The percentage of Negroes employed in all job classifications and found in the labor markets comprising these three SMSA's are shown on Tables 15, 16, and 17, respectively.

---

65. The Northeast includes firms with corporate headquarters in the following SMSA's only: New York, Philadelphia, Boston, Pittsburgh, Washington, D.C., Baltimore, Newark, Buffalo, Jersey City, and Rochester.

TABLE 14. *Trucking Industry*
Employment by Race, Occupation, and Firm Size
Northeast Region, 1968

Job Classifications	All Firms			Small Firms[a]			Large Firms[b]		
	Total	Negro	Percent Negro	Total	Negro	Percent Negro	Total	Negro	Percent Negro
Management	3,295	5	0.1	1,379	—	—	1,916	5	0.3
Road drivers	7,394	353	4.8	2,255	283	12.5	5,139	70	1.4
Local drivers	16,692	1,749	10.5	9,721	1,077	11.1	6,971	672	9.6
Dockmen	5,205	830	15.9	1,745	387	22.2	3,460	443	12.8
Mechanics	2,323	122	5.3	855	42	4.9	1,468	80	5.5
Oilers	234	111	47.4	22	22	100.0	212	89	42.0
Washers	138	109	79.0	22	22	100.0	116	87	75.0
Service workers	19	19	100.0	—	—	—	19	19	100.0
Dispatchers	1,182	—	—	539	—	—	643	—	—
Warehousemen	320	11	3.4	224	11	4.9	96	—	—
Helpers	2,423	792	32.7	1,803	395	21.9	620	397	64.0
Clerical workers	6,008	346	5.8	1,619	—	—	4,389	346	7.9
Male	747	31	4.1	143	—	—	604	31	5.1
Female	5,261	315	6.0	1,476	—	—	3,785	315	8.3
Total	45,233	4,447	9.8	20,184	2,239[c]	11.1	25,049	2,208[d]	8.8

Source: Data in author's possession.

Note: Data are based on Philadelphia, New York, and Boston SMSA's. See Appendixes A and B.

[a] Small firms are those having 100 or less employees.
[b] Large firms are those having 101 or more employees.
[c] Estimated Negroes—2,277 ($\pm$ 28.9 percent).
[d] Estimated Negroes—2,319 ($\pm$ 34.9 percent).

TABLE 15. *Trucking Industry*
Employment by Race, Occupation, and Firm Size
Philadelphia SMSA, 1968

Job Classifications	All Firms			Small Firms[a]			Large Firms[b]		
	Total	Negro	Percent Negro	Total	Negro	Percent Negro	Total	Negro	Percent Negro
Management	520	—	—	264	—	—	256	—	—
Road drivers	2,795	179	6.4	824	127	15.4	1,971	52	2.6
Local drivers	2,785	415	14.9	2,357	349	14.8	428	66	15.4
Dockmen	683	168	24.6	465	116	24.9	218	52	23.9
Mechanics	602	21	3.5	232	21	9.1	370	—	—
Oilers	59	59	100.0	11	11	100.0	48	48	100.0
Washers	120	54	45.0	11	11	100.0	109	43	39.4
Service workers	—	—	—	—	—	—	—	—	—
Dispatchers	125	—	—	106	—	—	19	—	—
Warehousemen	32	—	—	32	—	—	—	—	—
Helpers	35	—	—	21	—	—	14	—	—
Clerical workers	1,101	33	3.0	465	—	—	636	33	5.2
Male	195	23	11.8	53	—	—	142	23	16.2
Female	906	10	1.1	412	—	—	494	10	2.0
Total	8,857	929	10.5	4,788	635	13.3	4,069	294	7.2

Source: Data in author's possession.

[a] Small firms are those having 100 or less employees.

[b] Large firms are those having 101 or more employees.

TABLE 16. Trucking Industry
Employment by Race, Occupation, and Firm Size
New York SMSA, 1968

Job Classifications	All Firms			Small Firms[a]			Large Firms[b]		
	Total	Negro	Percent Negro	Total	Negro	Percent Negro	Total	Negro	Percent Negro
Management	1,239	5	0.4	454	—	—	785	5	0.6
Road drivers	600	—	—	600	—	—	600	—	—
Local drivers	6,700	874	13.0	2,820	279	9.9	3,880	595	15.3
Dockmen	2,359	509	21.6	444	134	30.2	3,880	375	19.6
Mechanics	666	70	10.5	196	—	—	1,915	70	14.9
Oilers	50	25	50.0	—	—	—	50	25	50.0
Washers	30	30	100.0	—	—	—	30	30	100.0
Service workers	20	20	100.0	—	—	—	20	20	100.0
Dispatchers	555	—	—	165	—	—	390	—	—
Warehousemen	121	10	8.3	21	10	47.6	100	—	—
Helpers	1,565	735	47.0	940	320	34.0	625	415	66.4
Clerical workers	2,212	270	12.2	382	—	—	1,830	270	14.7
Male	326	—	—	31	—	—	295	—	—
Female	1,886	270	14.3	351	—	—	1,535	270	17.6
Total	16,117	2,548	15.8	5,422	743	13.7	10,695	1,805	16.9

Source: Data in author's possession.

[a] Small firms are those having 100 or less employees.

[b] Large firms are those having 101 or more employees.

TABLE 17. *Trucking Industry*
Employment by Race, Occupation, and Firm Size
Boston SMSA, 1968

Job Classifications	All Firms			Small Firms[a]			Large Firms[b]		
	Total	Negro	Percent Negro	Total	Negro	Percent Negro	Total	Negro	Percent Negro
Management	424	—	—	120	—	—	304	—	—
Road drivers	924	10	1.1	220	10	4.5	704	—	—
Local drivers	1,637	25	1.5	640	20	3.1	997	5	0.5
Dockmen	606	5	0.8	110	—	—	496	5	1.0
Mechanics	252	5	2.0	60	—	—	192	5	2.6
Oilers	37	—	—	—	—	—	37	—	—
Washers	27	—	—	—	—	—	27	—	—
Service workers	—	—	—	—	—	—	—	—	—
Dispatchers	141	—	—	50	—	—	91	—	—
Warehousemen	50	—	—	50	—	—	—	—	—
Helpers	250	10	4.0	250	10	4.0	—	—	—
Clerical workers	751	16	2.3	90	—	—	661	16	2.4
Male	48	—	—	—	—	—	48	—	—
Female	703	16	2.3	90	—	—	613	16	2.6
Total	5,099	71	1.4	1,590	40	2.5	3,509	31	0.9

Source: Data in author's possession.

[a] Small firms are those having 100 or less employees.

[b] Large firms are those having 101 or more employees.

New York, with its polyglot population of nationalities, accounted for a larger proportion of Negro employees than the other two sample SMSA's used in this area. Even though the New York trucking firms' manpower is 15.8 percent Negro, a disproportionate number of Negroes were employed in the low-paying jobs or worked for special commodity haulers where the work is dirty and back breaking. Also, the numerous carriers hauling for New York's garment industry often employ teenage Negroes as sorters and checkers, but they pay them minimum wage rates for working after school and at night.

Boston accounted for the smallest percentage of Negro employees, not only among the three SMSA's in the Northeast, but among all thirteen SMSA's constituting the national sample. The one most significant factor explaining the poor showing in the Boston SMSA is that the Irish, as a group, have captured the industry and they also control the local Teamster unions. Boston had only 1.4 percent Negro employees in the trucking industry, but the nonwhite population for 1960 was only 3.4 percent. To understand Boston's poor posture, it is necessary to compare it with the difference found between the percentage of nonwhites in all sample SMSA's and the percentage of Negroes employed by the industry in these same SMSA's. This will be done later.

With the exceptions noted above, the Northeast is typical of the nation with reference to the occupational distribution of Negro employment. None of the participating firms were located in the heart of Negro neighborhoods. With the exception of those firms located outside the cities proper, companies interviewed in the Philadelphia, Boston, and New York SMSA's were more dependent upon the union as a source for employees than those in other areas of the country.

A larger percentage of female Negro clerical help was found in New York. Most of the clerical personnel employed in the other two SMSA's were white. Smaller firms have a tendency to employ more Negroes as dockmen, helpers, and local drivers than do the larger firms, but these small firms employed no female Negroes in clerical positions. Apparently the larger firms have at least one white employee willing to help a Negro secretary during the period of adjustment. In addition, the secretarial help in the smaller firms are a tightly-knit group often consisting of two or three secretaries who are friends or relatives.

Interestingly enough, when asked about Negro employment at terminal locations in cities other than the ones visited, all firms having such facilities in Baltimore and Washington pointed them out as cities where they employed more Negroes. They suggested this was due not only to the fact that proportionately more Negroes live in these cities but also because the makeup of the Teamster locals is different. Historically, no single ethnic group has dominated the locals in Baltimore or Washington, D.C., as they do in northern New Jersey, for example, where Italians have a grip on the local unions, or in Boston where the Irish are in control.

As might be expected, all of the sample firms were union companies. Several of the company representatives agreed that the industry as a whole is weak at the level of middle management, and this partially accounts for their inertia regarding the employment of more Negroes. They suggested, however, that the Teamsters share some of the responsibility for the small percentage of Negroes employed in the better-paying jobs and in particular as road drivers. They were extremely vague as to the degree union leaders could or would be willing to do something about removing or modifying hiring procedures which have worked against Negroes.

The smaller, poorly-managed firms, whether they had a high percentage of Negroes on their payrolls or not, immediately went on the defensive and told the author: "We never discriminated against anyone." "Why, even some of our best friends are Negroes." "The Irish, Italians, and Poles made it on their own. Why can't the Negroes?"

Representatives from the larger firms were somewhat more candid about equal employment problems. At the same time, no doubt fearing recrimination from the Teamsters, the representatives from the larger firms were unwilling to state categorically the degree to which the Teamsters are responsible for the various racial patterns of employment. They were willing to tell "horror stories" about the union, its leaders, and its unreasonable demands, but when it came to the topic of interest they talked in vaguer terms.

NEGRO EMPLOYMENT IN THE SOUTH

The four SMSA's comprising the sample areas for the southern region [66] of the country are: Birmingham, Charlotte, Atlanta,

---

66. The Southern firms with corporate headquarters in the following SMSA's only: Atlanta, Miami, New Orleans, Tampa, Louisville, Birmingham, Memphis, Charlotte, Norfolk, Winston-Salem Greensboro, Houston, Dallas, San Antonio, Fort Worth, and El Paso.

and the combined cities of Winston-Salem and Greensboro. Seven small firms and eight large firms made up the sample selected for the four combined SMSA's.

Prior to the Civil War, slaves in the South welcomed the opportunity to drive a wagon rather than labor with a hoe gang in the fields. Negro slaves hired out by owners to work in the towns were trained in many kinds of manual labor, including the driving of horse-drawn carts. During the Civil War, Negroes in the Union Forces were sometimes found to be more competent drivers than whites.[67] The dependence upon Negroes as draymen in the late nineteenth-century South laid the foundation upon which driving was viewed as a "Negro job." As motor vehicles replaced the horse-drawn carts and the work became less burdensome and dirty, whites moved into the driving occupations. This transition was gradual and imperceptible.

> When tractors and motor trucks are introduced, new "white men's jobs" are created out of old "Negro jobs" on the farm and in transportation. . . . Progress itself seems to work against the Negroes. When work becomes less heavy, less dirty, or less risky, Negroes are displaced. Old-fashioned, low-paying, inefficient enterprises, continually being driven out of competition, are often the only ones that employ much Negro labor.[68]

At present, there are no jobs in the trucking industry which are defined as "Negro jobs" by either the Teamsters or the industry. Two causes seem to have occasioned the fact that in the South "Negro jobs" have disappeared. The large unionized firms pay such high wage rates that these jobs are coveted by whites. Second, small nonunion firms, usually family owned, have a predominantly Negro work force with which whites as a rule refuse to work. Therefore, racial patterns of employment vary between union and nonunion firms.

Technological changes on the platform, which made the tasks once performed by Negro dockmen less heavy, pushed some Negroes out of these jobs. Prior to the 1950's, for example, many terminals hired Negroes as dockmen, but the checkers were ex-

---

67. Bell Irvin Wiley, *Southern Negroes 1861-1865* (New Haven: Yale University Press, 1938), p. 111.

68. Arnold Rose, *The Negro in America* (Boston: The Beacon Press, 1956), p. 69. This work is a condensation of Gunnar Myrdal's classic work, *The American Dilemma.*

clusively white. The introduction of front-end fork lifts and
other mechanical devices reduced dependence on strong backs to
move and separate freight on the platform. The Teamsters got
a substantial increase for their checkers, which led employers to
change the work assignments on the platforms. The white checkers were given jobs on the new equipment and the Negro dockmen were discharged. The employers said illiterate Negroes
might have been able to learn how to handle the new equipment,
but they were not able to read and record the bills of lading.
There is no evidence that the Teamsters had sought the wage
increases primarily to displace the Negroes, for it is in keeping
with the IBT's objectives to gain for its members higher wages
with improved working conditions. In any event, the results were
much the same as in the past: Negroes were displaced with
the advent of new technologies.

As Table 18 shows, there is a higher percentage of Negroes
employed by the southern domiciled truckers than there is by
firms in the Northeast section of the country. When the four
SMSA's in the South are viewed independently, the percentage of
Negroes in each is as follows: Winston-Salem Greensboro, 7.0
percent (Table 19) ; Birmingham, 25.2 percent (Table 20) ; Charlotte, 16.2 percent (Table 21) ; Atlanta, 10.8 percent (Table 22).
In the Northeast, 9.8 percent of all employees are Negroes, while
in the South, 15.0 percent of the employees are Negroes. In
isolation, these data seem to indicate that the South is less discriminatory than other areas of the country, but this is not the
case. In the South the small firms employ 3,557 or 59.8 percent
of the total 5,942 Negroes working there. It is estimated that
over one-half of the firms in Birmingham are nonunion. The pay
scale for drivers is approximately $2.50 an hour for a fifty-hour
week in these nonunion firms. Therefore, the presence of a high
percentage of Negroes in the South is caused not by the southern
employer's desire for equal employment, but rather by the fact
that Negro labor is cheaper and that sometimes Negroes are
employed to keep the unions out.

The trucking industry arrived on the southern scene later than
it did in other parts of the country, and the South was the last
part of the country to be unionized by the Teamsters. When
trucking started to garner the long haul work, the IBT was able
to organize the South by means of secondary boycotts and later

TABLE 18. Trucking Industry

Employment by Race, Occupation, and Firm Size
South Region, 1968

Job Classifications	All Firms			Small Firms[a]			Large Firms[b]		
	Total	Negro	Percent Negro	Total	Negro	Percent Negro	Total	Negro	Percent Negro
Management	2,791	—	—	504	—	—	2,287	—	—
Road drivers	16,411	702	4.3	3,386	566	16.7	13,025	136	1.0
Local drivers	6,183	2,501	40.4	3,195	2,197	68.8	2,988	304	10.2
Dockmen	3,640	1,360	37.4	305	283	92.8	3,335	1,077	32.3
Mechanics	3,112	404	13.0	465	137	29.5	2,647	267	10.1
Oilers	120	120	100.0	61	61	100.0	120	120	100.0
Washers	220	220	100.0	178	89	50.0	159	159	100.0
Service workers	496	367	74.0	192	—	—	318	278	87.4
Dispatchers	640	—	—	—	—	—	448	—	—
Warehousemen	—	—	—	—	—	—	—	—	—
Helpers	474	224	47.3	474	224	47.3	—	—	—
Clerical workers	5,609	44	0.8	829	—	—	4,780	44	0.9
Male	78	10	12.8	61	—	—	17	10	58.8
Female	5,531	34	0.6	768	—	—	4,763	34	0.7
Total	39,696	5,942	15.0	9,589	3,557[c]	37.1	30,107	2,385[d]	7.9

Source: Data in author's possession.

Note: Data are based on Burmingham, Charlotte, Atlanta, and Winston-Salem Greensboro SMSA's. See Appendixes A and B.

[a] Small firms are those with 100 or less employees.
[b] Large firms are those with 101 or more employees.
[c] Estimated Negroes—3,938 (27.1 percent).
[d] Estimated Negroes—3,008 (16.5 percent).

TABLE 19. Trucking Industry
Employment by Race, Occupation, and Firm Size
Winston-Salem Greensboro SMSA, 1968

Job Classifications	All Firms			Small Firms[a]			Large Firms[b]		
	Total	Negro	Percent Negro	Total	Negro	Percent Negro	Total	Negro	Percent Negro
Management	386	—	—	18	—	—	368	—	—
Road drivers	2,546	19	0.7	96	9	9.4	2,450	10	0.4
Local drivers	328	19	5.8	48	12	25.0	280	7	2.5
Dockmen	593	181	30.5	15	6	40.0	578	175	30.3
Mechanics	928	35	3.8	18	—	—	910	35	3.9
Oilers	105	105	100.0	—	—	—	105	105	100.0
Washers	—	—	—	—	—	—	—	—	—
Service workers	61	61	100.0	9	9	100.0	52	52	100.0
Dispatchers	95	—	—	15	—	—	80	—	—
Warehousemen	—	—	—	—	—	—	—	—	—
Helpers	—	—	—	—	—	—	—	—	—
Clerical workers	1,125	14	1.2	15	—	—	1,110	14	1.3
Male	4	4	100.0	—	—	—	4	4	100.0
Female	1,121	10	0.9	15	—	—	1,106	10	0.9
Total	6,167	434	7.0	234	36	15.4	5,933	398	6.7

Source: Data in author's possession.

[a] Small firms are those having 100 or less employees.

[b] Large firms are those having 101 or more employees.

TABLE 20. *Trucking Industry*

Employment by Race, Occupation, and Firm Size

Birmingham SMSA, 1968

Job Classifications	All Firms			Small Firms[a]			Large Firms[b]		
	Total	Negro	Percent Negro	Total	Negro	Percent Negro	Total	Negro	Percent Negro
Management	311	—	—	55	—	—	256	—	—
Road drivers	1,507	136	9.0	187	132	70.6	1,320	4	0.3
Local drivers	955	625	65.4	715	605	84.6	240	20	8.3
Dockmen	—	—	—	—	—	—	—	—	—
Mechanics	153	35	22.9	33	11	33.3	120	24	20.0
Oilers	—	—	—	—	—	—	—	—	—
Washers	62	62	100.0	22	22	100.0	40	40	100.0
Service workers	48	40	83.3	—	—	—	48	40	83.3
Dispatchers	55	—	—	11	—	—	44	—	—
Warehousemen	—	—	—	—	—	—	—	—	—
Helpers	—	—	—	—	—	—	—	—	—
Clerical workers	466	—	—	66	—	—	400	—	—
Male	22	—	—	22	—	—	—	—	—
Female	444	—	—	44	—	—	400	—	—
Total	3,557	898	25.2	1,089	770	70.7	2,468	128	5.2

Source: Data in author's possession.

[a] Small firms are those having 100 or less employees.

[b] Large firms are those having 101 or more employees.

TABLE 21. *Trucking Industry*
Employment by Race, Occupation, and Firm Size
Charlotte SMSA, 1968

Job Classifications	All Firms			Small Firms[a]			Large Firms[b]		
	Total	Negro	Percent Negro	Total	Negro	Percent Negro	Total	Negro	Percent Negro
Management	330	—	—	90	—	—	240	—	—
Road drivers	2,092	80	3.8	680	40	5.9	1,412	40	2.8
Local drivers	684	190	27.8	160	150	93.8	524	40	7.6
Dockmen	856	412	48.1	120	120	100.0	736	292	39.7
Mechanics	512	64	12.5	100	—	—	412	64	15.5
Oilers	—	—	—	—	—	—	—	—	—
Washers	—	—	—	—	—	—	—	—	—
Service workers	94	54	57.4	70	30	42.9	24	24	100.0
Dispatchers	100	—	—	40	—	—	60	—	—
Warehousemen	—	—	—	—	—	—	—	—	—
Helpers	180	100	55.6	180	100	55.6	—	—	—
Clerical workers	770	8	1.0	130	—	—	640	8	1.3
Male	—	—	—	—	—	—	—	—	—
Female	770	8	1.0	130	—	—	640	8	1.3
Total	5,618	908	16.2	1,570	440	28.0	4,048	468	11.6

Source: Data in author's possession.

[a] Small firms are those having 100 or less employees.

[b] Large firms are those having 101 or more employees.

TABLE 22. *Trucking Industry*
Employment by Race, Occupation, and Firm Size
Atlanta SMSA, 1968

Job Classifications	All Firms			Small Firms[a]			Large Firms[b]		
	Total	Negro	Percent Negro	Total	Negro	Percent Negro	Total	Negro	Percent Negro
Management	195	—	—	45	—	—	150	—	—
Road drivers	1,325	50	3.8	450	38	8.4	875	12	1.4
Local drivers	587	123	21.0	315	68	21.6	272	55	20.2
Dockmen	488	120	24.6	—	—	—	488	120	24.6
Mechanics	170	47	27.6	45	45	100.0	125	2	1.6
Oilers	—	—	—	—	—	—	—	—	—
Washers	8	5	62.5	—	—	—	8	5	62.5
Service workers	40	—	—	15	—	—	25	—	—
Dispatchers	—	—	—	—	—	—	—	—	—
Warehousemen	—	—	—	—	—	—	—	—	—
Helpers	30	—	—	30	—	—	—	—	—
Clerical workers	397	5	1.3	135	—	—	262	5	1.9
Male	5	2	40.0	—	—	—	5	2	40.0
Female	392	3	0.8	135	—	—	257	3	1.2
Total	3,240	350	10.8	1,035	151	14.6	2,205	199	9.0

Source: Data in author's possession.

[a] Small firms are those having 100 or less employees.

[b] Large firms are those having 101 or more employees.

by "hot cargo clauses" [69] in the contracts. Unlike other urban areas in the country, there are no hiring halls found in southern cities. In theory, the southern employers thus are freer to hire whomover they desire—including Negro road drivers. In practice, the Teamsters in the South can still exercise enough indirect control through other devices to keep Negroes out. Most likely, any union official in the South who would side with the employer in the hiring of Negroes would be voted out of office by the white majority. Ironically, the Southern Conference of Teamsters, the smallest of the Conferences, is growing faster than any of the other three conferences. Yet, the Southern Conference's increased membership is coming from small manufacturing firms where many of the employees are Negroes. The dilemma facing the Teamsters is that as they try to organize Negroes working for nontrucking firms in the South, they must project a nondiscriminatory image, but at the same time they cannot afford to incur the wrath of the white members employed by the trucking industry.

NEGRO EMPLOYMENT IN THE MIDWEST

Detroit, Chicago, and St. Louis are the three SMSA's comprising the sample areas for the Midwest.[70] Of the thirty-four companies constituting the sample firms in these three SMSA's, seventeen were large firms, while the remaining seventeen were small.

In the Midwest all firms interviewed were union companies. This is not only the very heartland of the trucking industry, but the very area in which Farrell Dobbs first organized the road drivers. It was from this geographical base that the union reached out and subsequently organized the road drivers throughout the country. The union enjoys a long history of strength in

---

69. Basically, where "hot cargo clauses" are included in the contracts it means union members will not handle goods hauled by a nonunion carrier. If a nonunion firm does not serve the point of destination because his operating rights do not permit it, he must interchange the freight with another carrier. Therefore, southern firms must depend on companies throughout the country with whom they interchange freight. This technique enabled Hoffa to bludgeon the southern firms into capitulating and accepting a union shop.

70. The Midwest includes those firms with corporate headquarters in the following SMSA's only: Chicago, Detroit, St. Louis, Cleveland, Minneapolis and St. Paul, Milwaukee, Cincinnati, Indianapolis, Dayton, Columbus, Akron, and Toledo.

this area, which is reflected in the employers blaming the union for the industry's refusal to hire more Negroes. It seems that those earlier and much more turbulent years of the Teamsters in Detroit and Chicago have scared the industry more in this area than some other areas.

Ethnic blocs in Detroit and Chicago, while not as easily distinguishable as the Irish in Boston, dominate many of the better-paying jobs. This phenomenon, in conjunction with the indifference and inability of union leaders to control the rank and file, partially accounts for the relatively few Negroes employed in this area. Table 23 shows that in the twelve SMSA's included in this study located in the Midwest, only 4.6 percent of all employees are Negroes. In the South, smaller nonunion firms accounted for a larger percentage of Negroes, whereas in the Midwest the difference between the percentage of Negroes employed by large and small firms is insignificant. The attitude that other minority groups were able to pull themselves up by their bootstraps is a recurring theme. Yet employers concede that, historically, Negroes have never found it easy to get the better-paying jobs available in the industry. Formerly located behind the stockyards of Chicago, companies were able to find an ample supply of labor among the Polish and other ethnic groups living "behind the yards." As the companies moved their terminal locations to such places as Cicero and its environs, Negroes were afraid to look for employment in these all-white enclaves. In addition, employers still relied on informal referrals and union officials as a means of making job vacancies known. The clerical help in this area is also predominantly white. Tables 24, 25, and 26 show this job classification and others for the three SMSA's used in this area separately.

NEGRO EMPLOYMENT IN THE WEST

Denver, San Francisco, and Los Angeles are the three sample areas of the West.[71] Company representatives from thirty firms having corporate headquarters in these three SMSA's were interviewed—twelve were large firms; eighteen were small. The percentage of Negroes employed in all job classifications for firms having corporate headquarters in forty-eight SMSA's throughout

---

71. The West includes those firms with corporate headquarters in the following SMSA's only: Denver, Seattle and Portland, Phoenix, Los Angeles, San Diego, Oklahoma City, Kansas City, and Omaha.

TABLE 23. Trucking Industry
Employment by Race, Occupation, and Firm Size
Midwest Region, 1968

Job Classifications	All Firms			Small Firms[a]			Large Firms[b]		
	Total	Negro	Percent Negro	Total	Negro	Percent Negro	Total	Negro	Percent Negro
Management	3,829	—	—	1,437	—	—	2,392	—	—
Road drivers	19,115	214	1.1	6,520	93	1.4	12,595	121	1.0
Local drivers	20,936	1,146	5.5	7,277	483	6.6	13,659	663	4.9
Dockmen	16,456	947	5.8	2,125	538	25.3	14,331	409	2.9
Mechanics	3,390	249	7.3	1,102	—	—	2,288	249	10.9
Oilers	—	—	—	—	—	—	—	—	—
Washers	287	263	91.6	29	29	100.0	258	234	90.7
Service workers	626	331	52.9	91	91	100.0	535	240	44.9
Dispatchers	1,499	—	—	414	—	—	1,085	—	—
Warehousemen	386	89	23.1	188	32	17.0	198	57	28.8
Helpers	3,536	186	5.3	1,754	—	—	1,782	186	10.4
Clerical workers	6,523	63	1.0	1,701	—	—	4,822	63	1.3
Male	577	—	—	85	—	—	492	—	—
Female	5,946	63	1.1	1,616	—	—	4,330	63	1.5
Total	76,583	3,488	4.6	22,638	1,266[c]	5.6	53,945	2,222[d]	4.1

Source: Data in author's possession.

Note: Data are based on Chicago, St. Louis, and Detroit SMSA's. See Appendixes A and B.

a Small firms are those having 100 or less employees.

b Large firms are those having 101 or more employees.

c Estimated Negroes—1,482 (±28.5 percent).

d Estimated Negroes—2,215 (±13.6 percent).

TABLE 24. *Trucking Industry*
Employment by Race, Occupation, and Firm Size
Chicago SMSA, 1968

Job Classifications	All Firms			Small Firms[a]			Large Firms[b]		
	Total	Negro	Percent Negro	Total	Negro	Percent Negro	Total	Negro	Percent Negro
Management	796	—	—	396	—	—	400	—	—
Road drivers	1,571	26	1.7	1,327	21	1.6	244	5	2.0
Local drivers	8,727	571	6.5	2,568	25	8.8	6,159	346	5.6
Dockmen	1,215	181	14.9	610	118	19.3	605	63	10.4
Mechanics	1,165	210	18.0	257	—	—	908	210	23.1
Oilers	—	—	—	—	—	—	—	—	—
Washers	52	52	100.0	32	32	100.0	20	20	100.0
Service workers	215	112	52.1	—	—	—	215	112	52.1
Dispatchers	442	—	—	139	—	—	303	—	—
Warehousemen	—	—	—	—	—	—	—	—	—
Helpers	1,559	107	6.9	107	—	—	1,452	107	7.4
Clerical workers	2,206	15	0.7	449	—	—	1,757	15	0.8
Male	59	—					59	—	
Female	2,147	15	0.7	449	—	—	1,698	15	0.9
Total	17,948	1,274	7.1	5,885	396	6.7	12,063	878	7.3

Source: Data in author's possession.

[a] Small firms are those having 100 or less employees.

[b] Large firms are those having 101 or more employees.

TABLE 25. Trucking Industry
Employment by Race, Occupation, and Firm Size
St. Louis SMSA, 1968

Job Classifications	All Firms			Small Firms[a]			Large Firms[b]		
	Total	Negro	Percent Negro	Total	Negro	Percent Negro	Total	Negro	Percent Negro
Management	397	—	—	105	—	—	292	—	—
Road drivers	1,689	32	1.9	578	21	3.6	1,111	11	1.0
Local drivers	1,204	123	10.2	368	79	21.5	836	44	5.3
Dockmen	3,349	194	5.8	280	122	43.6	3,069	72	2.3
Mechanics	240	—	—	70	—	—	170	—	—
Oilers	—	—	—	—	—	—	—	—	—
Washers	—	—	—	—	—	—	—	—	—
Service workers	42	26	61.9	26	26	100.0	16	—	—
Dispatchers	139	—	—	35	—	—	104	—	—
Warehousemen	29	20	69.0	18	9	50.0	11	11	100.0
Helpers	—	—	—	—	—	—	—	—	—
Clerical workers	527	11	2.1	131	—	—	396	11	2.8
Male	—	—	—	—	—	—	—	—	—
Female	527	11	2.1	131	—	—	396	11	2.8
Total	7,616	406	5.3	1,611	257	16.0	6,005	149	2.5

Source: Data in author's possession.

[a] Small firms are those having 100 or less employees.

[b] Large firms are those having 101 or more employees.

TABLE 26. Trucking Industry
Employment by Race, Occupation, and Firm Size
Detroit SMSA, 1968

Job Classifications	All Firms			Small Firms[a]			Large Firms[b]		
	Total	Negro	Percent Negro	Total	Negro	Percent Negro	Total	Negro	Percent Negro
Management	466	—	—	142	—	—	324	—	—
Road drivers	4,195	32	0.8	658	—	—	3,537	32	0.9
Local drivers	2,056	32	1.6	733	—	—	1,323	32	2.4
Dockmen	511	16	3.1	117	—	—	394	16	4.1
Mechanics	357	—	—	125	—	—	232	—	—
Oilers	—	—	—	—	—	—	—	—	—
Washers	108	97	89.8	—	—	—	108	97	89.8
Service workers	98	49	50.0	—	—	—	98	49	50.0
Dispatchers	168	—	—	33	—	—	135	—	—
Warehousemen	95	5	5.3	25	—	—	70	5	7.1
Helpers	360	27	7.5	333	—	—	27	27	100.0
Clerical workers	669	—	—	167	—	—	502	—	—
Male	211	—	—	17	—	—	194	—	—
Female	458	—	—	150	—	—	308	—	—
Total	9,083	258	2.8	2,333	—	—	6,750	258	3.8

Source: Data in author's possession.

[a] Small firms are those having 100 or less employees.

[b] Large firms are those having 101 or more employees.

the country is 7.6 percent, while the West, as Table 27 shows, has a 4.4 percent Negro work force. When the three sample SMSA's in the West are viewed independently, the percentage of Negroes employed in each is as follows: Denver, 3.1 percent; San Francisco, 5.3 percent; and Los Angeles, 4.9 percent. The percentage of Negroes found in the various job classifications within the labor markets comprising these three SMSA's are shown in Tables 28, 29, and 30.

Although all participating firms were signatories to collective bargaining agreements negotiated by the Teamsters, the degree of union control over the hiring of employees differed from firm to firm. In other parts of the country, a strong local union usually does not exercise the same degree of power over all companies; some firms, because of past practices, or because of the nature of their operations, are not compelled to do all their hiring through union sources. In the West, all the smaller firms seemed to be more dependent upon the union for new drivers than were companies of similar size in other parts of the country. This partially explains why the smaller firms do not employ substantially more Negroes than the larger firms.

Many firms in the West blamed the Teamsters for discriminatory practices. For example, Teamster Local 85 in San Francisco, according to employers, has only a few Negro members. Employers attribute the absence of Negroes in this local to racial attitudes harbored by the rank and file, and not to biases or policies fostered by the union leaders. The industry representatives explicitly stated that unless Teamster officials convince the business agents and shop stewards that the union welcomes all—regardless of race—integration in the trucking industry is nothing more than a wishful hope. Indeed, these employer sentiments were expressed in other areas of the country, but they were stated in stronger terms in the West, and in the San Francisco area in particular.

On a regional basis, 4.4 percent of employees in the western SMSA's were Negro. Employers conceded that their terminals outside this area do not employ proportionately more Negroes. One employer stated that the most difficult jobs in which to place Negroes are clerical positions in their southern terminals. As was true of firms throughout the nation, those with corporate headquarters in the West demand different standards for similar jobs, and use diverse hiring and screening procedures. One company preferred that road drivers be over forty years old, in contrast to the 25-35 year age range preferred by most employers.

TABLE 27. *Trucking Industry*
Employment by Race, Occupation, and Firm Size
West Region, 1968

Job Classifications	All Firms			Small Firms[a]			Large Firms[b]		
	Total	Negro	Percent Negro	Total	Negro	Percent Negro	Total	Negro	Percent Negro
Management	4,422	8	0.2	1,433	—	—	2,989	8	0.3
Road drivers	16,967	148	0.9	7,508	95	1.3	9,459	53	0.6
Local drivers	10,109	469	4.6	5,409	220	4.1	4,700	249	5.3
Dockmen	6,035	831	13.8	1,739	494	28.4	4,296	337	7.8
Mechanics	4,226	—	—	954	—	—	3,272	—	—
Oilers	—	—	—	—	—	—	—	—	—
Washers	204	194	95.1	94	94	100.0	110	100	90.9
Service workers	1,423	397	27.9	182	120	65.9	1,241	277	22.3
Dispatchers	949	8	0.8	430	—	—	519	8	1.5
Warehousemen	—	—	—	—	—	—	—	—	—
Helpers	126	37	29.4	31	—	—	95	37	38.9
Clerical workers	5,266	85	1.6	1,324	—	—	3,942	85	2.2
Male	369	12	3.3	51	—	—	318	12	3.8
Female	4,896	73	1.5	1,273	—	—	3,623	73	2.0
Total	49,727	2,177	4.4	19,104	1,023[c]	5.4	30,623	1,154[c]	3.8

Source: Data in author's possession.

Note: Data are based on Denver, San Francisco, and Los Angeles SMSA's. See Appendixes A and B.

[a] Small firms are those having 100 or less employees.
[b] Large firms are those having 101 or more employees.
[c] Estimated Negroes—984 (±19.6 percent).
[d] Estimated Negroes—1,112 (±17.5 percent).

TABLE 28. *Trucking Industry*
Employment by Race, Occupation, and Firm Size
Denver SMSA, 1968

Job Classifications	All Firms			Small Firms[a]			Large Firms[b]		
	Total	Negro	Percent Negro	Total	Negro	Percent Negro	Total	Negro	Percent Negro
Management	888	4	0.5	72	—	—	816	4	0.5
Road drivers	3,008	4	0.1	816	—	—	2,192	4	0.2
Local drivers	964	20	2.1	360	16	4.4	604	4	0.7
Dockmen	960	64	6.7	96	32	33.3	864	32	3.7
Mechanics	800	—	—	96	—	—	704	—	—
Oilers	—	—	—	—	—	—	—	—	—
Washers	16	16	100.0	16	16	100.0	—	—	—
Service workers	288	132	45.8	—	—	—	288	132	45.8
Dispatchers	92	4	4.3	32	—	—	60	4	6.7
Warehousemen	—	—	—	—	—	—	—	—	—
Helpers	—	—	—	—	—	—	—	—	—
Clerical workers	1,292	12	0.9	88	—	—	1,204	12	1.0
Male	116	—	—	—	—	—	116	—	—
Female	1,176	12	1.0	88	—	—	1,088	12	1.1
Total	8,308	256	3.1	1,576	64	4.1	6,732	192	2.9

Source: Data in author's possession.

[a] Small firms are those having 100 or less employees.

[b] Large firms are those having 101 or more employees.

TABLE 29. *Trucking Industry*
Employment by Race, Occupation, and Firm Size
San Francisco SMSA, 1968

Job Classifications	All Firms			Small Firms[a]			Large Firms[b]		
	Total	Negro	Percent Negro	Total	Negro	Percent Negro	Total	Negro	Percent Negro
Management	682	—	—	244	—	—	438	—	—
Road drivers	2,372	28	1.2	1,128	19	1.7	1,244	9	0.7
Local drivers	2,711	65	2.4	1,015	28	2.8	1,696	37	2.2
Dockmen	2,058	365	17.7	310	122	39.4	1,748	243	13.9
Mechanics	850	—	—	132	—	—	718	—	—
Oilers	—	—	—	—	—	—	—	—	—
Washers	—	—	—	—	—	—	—	—	—
Service workers	89	38	42.7	56	38	67.9	33	—	—
Dispatchers	145	—	—	47	—	—	98	—	—
Warehousemen	—	—	—	—	—	—	—	—	—
Helpers	—	—	—	—	—	—	—	—	—
Clerical workers	658	9	1.4	197	—	—	461	9	2.0
Male	33	5	15.2	—	—	—	33	5	15.2
Female	625	4	0.6	197	—	—	428	4	0.9
Total	9,565	505	5.3	3,129	207	6.6	6,436	298	4.6

Source: Data in author's possession.

[a] Small firms are those having 100 or less employees.
[b] Large firms are those having 101 or more employees.

TABLE 30. Trucking Industry
Employment by Race, Occupation, and Firm Size
Los Angeles SMSA, 1968

Job Classifications	All Firms			Small Firms[a]			Large Firms[b]		
	Total	Negro	Percent Negro	Total	Negro	Percent Negro	Total	Negro	Percent Negro
Management	1,116	—	—	546	—	—	570	—	—
Road drivers	3,580	76	2.1	1,155	52	4.5	2,425	24	1.0
Local drivers	2,635	219	8.3	1,418	84	5.9	1,217	135	11.1
Dockmen	1,153	92	8.0	588	63	10.7	565	29	5.1
Mechanics	949	—	—	210	—	—	739	—	—
Oilers									
Washers	93	93	100.0	21	21	100.0	72	72	100.0
Service workers	448	32	7.1	52	32	61.5	396	—	—
Dispatchers	376	—	—	178			198	—	—
Warehousemen									
Helpers	94	24	25.5	32	—	—	62	24	38.7
Clerical workers	1,119	34	3.0	472	—	—	647	34	5.3
Male	81	5	6.2	52	—	—	29	5	17.2
Female	1,038	29	2.8	420	—	—	618	29	4.7
Total	11,563	570	4.9	4,672	252	5.4	6,891	318	4.6

Source: Data in author's possession.

[a] Small firms are those having 100 or less employees.

[b] Large firms are those having 101 or more employees.

A representative from one of the larger carriers in the West acknowledged that separate seniority lists have a tendency to lock Negroes into the poorer-paying jobs because Negroes are less likely to transfer from the local driver's seniority list to the bottom of the over-the-road list. But this company representative indicated that separate seniority lists afforded terminal managers a well-defined specialized work group which the industry preferred. Yet, he believed the industry eventually will have to re-evaluate the use of separate seniority lists if Negroes are to gain admission into the higher paying jobs.

Prior to 1965, the federal government had done virtually nothing to persuade either the trucking industry or the Teamsters to grant Negroes equal employment opportunities. Yet, equal employment was a public policy as early as 1941. Recent legal, social, and political changes have enabled the federal government to inquire into the trucking industry's racial employment policies and practices. We now turn to these inquiries and the industry's response.

CHAPTER VI

Government Equal Opportunity Action and Industry Response

Beginning with Franklin D. Roosevelt in 1941, each succeeding president has issued executive orders intended to encourage government contractors to grant Negroes equal employment opportunities.[72] All of these presidential proclamations demand, as a minimal requirement, the inclusion of a nondiscrimination clause in federal contracts. The first Kennedy Order, No. 10925, March 6, 1961, also stipulated that contractors must "take affirmative action to ensure the applicants are employed and that employees are treated during employment without regard to their race, creed, color or national origin."[73] This was the first use of the "affirmative action" doctrine—the implication that complaint proceedings for alleged claims of discrimination were secondary to a company's obligation to reach out into the nation's labor markets to find qualified Negroes.

As a consequence of Executive Order 10925, the General Counsel of the Post Office Department was assigned the responsibility of handling all complaints arising where companies had contracts with the Post Office Department. The Department did have numerous contracts with truckers who hauled mail, but the majority of these were with small contract carriers employing relatively few people. In practice, postal inspectors incurred the responsibility of investigating complaints of alleged discrimination in hiring and upgrading. Although postal inspectors handled these complaints in a rather cursory manner, they performed this function until April 1964. Insofar as the trucking industry is

---

72. President Roosevelt's Executive Order No. 8802, June 25, 1941, covered only defense contractors, while his second Order No. 9346, May 29, 1943, covered all government contractors. In subsequent years the following orders were promulgated: President Truman's No. 10308, December 3, 1951; President Eisenhower's No. 10499, August 13, 1953; President Kennedy's Orders Nos. 10925, March 6, 1961 and 11114, June 22, 1963; and President Johnson's No. 11246, September 24, 1965.

73. Executive Order No. 10925, Section 301.

concerned, however, there was little actual government compliance activity prior to the second Executive Order of President Kennedy in 1963.

On June 22, 1963, President Kennedy modified his former order when he issued Executive Order 11114.[74] The chief difference between the second order and the first regarding the trucking industry was that the latter specified that a bill of lading bound the carrier to the terms of the Executive Order. Although a normal contract had to be in an amount of at least $10,000 before the government could inquire about a company's employment practices, no minimum applied to a bill of lading. This brought the trucking industry under the executive orders in a comprehensive manner for the first time.

In the event a company had contracts with more than one federal agency, each federal agency could conduct an investigation and the business community pointed out that this resulted in duplication of effort and cost. In an effort to minimize the bureaucratic red tape, the government assigned different industries to specific agencies. In April 1964, the Post Office Department, which had more business contacts with the railroads and motor carriers than did any other agency, was designated the Predominant Interest Agency (PIA) for investigating the minority employment practices in the transportation industry. At this time, Paul Nagle, a former administrative vice president of the United Federation of Postal Clerks, was named Deputy Contracts Compliance Officer. The authority to conduct compliance reviews was transferred from the Office of the General Counsel of the Post Office Department to the Office of Regional Administration, and compliance investigations began in earnest in the trucking industry.

INVESTIGATION AND RESPONSE

Nagle hired a staff and began a pilot study of the firms headquartered in the Charlotte, North Carolina area. The examiners discovered that, with rare exception, Negroes were not employed in clerical positions or as road drivers. They were, however, employed as warehousemen, dock workers, and in some instances as

---

74. The Order entitled, "Extending the Authority of the President's Committee on Equal Employment" did not substantially change the substance of Executive Order 10925, but it extended the government's jurisdiction to include federally assisted construction programs.

city drivers. Although approximately one-half of the companies
had sleeper cab operations, no Negroes were employed in this job
classification. One nonunion firm had thirty Negro road drivers,
but it did not operate sleeper cab vans. As the Department's contract compliance examiners expanded their efforts geographically,
they discovered that the Charlotte area was representative of
other areas of the country.

Another consistent phenomenon was that no company appeared
ready to alter its hiring and upgrading procedures. The companies domiciled in the Charlotte area requested that they be ex-
cused from undertaking individual and independent action in
integrating their sleeper cab operations. The Post Office Department believed that the issuance of sleeping bags by each company
might minimize the opposition for white drivers. This has not
been tried, partly because of the cost to the companies, and it is
extremely doubtful that it would work. The Department also fa-
vored the hiring of Negro employees in teams, which would have
eliminated, for the present, having Negro and white drivers
working together in close quarters for extended periods of time.
Most employers, however, fearing the reaction of the IBT and
not wanting to establish a precedent that might hinder their
freedom in assigning drivers, rejected this means of integrating
sleeper cab operations.

The IBT immediately opposed all Post Office Department recommendations to overcome some of the human problems that
might arise should companies hire Negro road drivers. What
aroused the ire of the rank and file was a rumor that the Department would "blackball" any driver leaving a firm because it
integrated its sleeper cabs. In vain, the Department tried to in-
form Teamster officials that this rumor, which began in the
Charlotte area, had absolutely no basis in fact. Ultimately, because southern locals allegedly objected to the hiring of "so many"
Negroes, Hoffa communicated with Paul Nagle to object to the
government's attempt at integrating sleeper cab operations.[75]

Hoffa made two points: (1) he defended the industry and
maintained that no employer ever denied Negroes employment,
and (2) he stated categorically that he would never allow any
firm to hire drivers under any arrangement other than what was
stipulated in the National Master Freight Agreement. Hoffa
warned Nagle that if a single company hired a Negro driver be-

---

75. This section is based upon interviews conducted with Post Office and
    company officials.

cause of government pressure, he would call a strike. "Not a wheel would turn," said Hoffa, and "the government could give its business to a wheelbarrow." He suggested that the Post Office Department would do better to investigate its own practice of giving business to every farmer and "hay shaker" who can afford a "broken down truck."

The Post Office Department at first relied primarily on conciliation and persuasion in an attempt to have the industry hire Negro over-the-road drivers. Neither the IBT nor the industry, however, was willing to alter the status quo even slightly. On March 9, 1965, Paul Nagle addressed the American Trucking Associations' Industrial Relations Committee.[76] The tone and content of this speech, and the questions raised by industry representatives afford an excellent insight into the stance of government and industry on equal employment objectives.

Nagle explained to the company representatives the distinction between the intent of the Civil Rights Act of 1964 and the objectives of contract compliance programs, hoping that a mutually agreeable program could be worked out. Although he believed that all individual complaints should and could be handled by the Equal Employment Opportunity Commission, Nagle interpreted complaints as a sign that his office and the industry had failed in a mutual undertaking. Ironically, as the Post Office Department tried to integrate the sleeper cab operations—perhaps the most difficult hiring and upgrading practice to change—Nagle idealistically assumed that the industry intended to cooperate fully. For example, he told the meeting:

Assuming that you as corporate officer were to learn that action is being taken against you under Title VII, we would if we knew of it attempt to help you with the Equal Employment Opportunity Commission in Washington and to have the issue resolved.[77]

The implication was that if the Department's report to the President's Committee was favorable, then it would be impossible for EEOC to sustain adverse action under Title VII. Nagle contended that the Department believed it was responsible for seeing that the Teamsters' Union did not discriminate where informal referral and hiring hall systems prevailed, although by the terms of the order the Department had no authority over the

---

76. Remarks of Paul A. Nagle before the ATA's Industrial Relations Com-

77. *Ibid.*
mittee, March 9, 1965, Miami Beach, Florida.

unions. Companies were reminded that Form 38, a notice sent to labor unions to notify them of a company's nondiscrimination policy, was still mandatory. Nagle suggested that companies ask the union to respond by mail indicating the union's understanding of the significance of Form 38. Should the IBT call a strike because of integration efforts on the part of the companies, firm representatives were guaranteed that the Department would go directly to the top union leaders.

The industry was assured that the Post Office Department would respect all reasonable tests used to screen employees. "Reasonable" was interpreted to mean that the tests would be acceptable to the government, as long as they were not structured primarily to exclude minorities. Company policies against nepotism likewise were to be respected by the government. In the event an impasse arose between the Department and the industry over hiring practices or possible sanctions, the President's Committee, then responsible for administering the executive order, had the power to make the final judgment.

Impact on Industry

Mr. Nagle's conciliatory approach made no clearly visible change in the industry's or union's attitudes toward opening up more long haul trucking jobs to Negroes. The white-Negro employment patterns existing in 1965 did not radically change. Some personnel directors, safety directors, and industrial relations people since then have gained the support of top management at the highest echelons and have honestly tried to employ more Negroes, but this is the exception and certainly not the rule. The fear of union reprisals, the economic consequences of a rebellious white rank and file, and deep antigovernment sentiments caused most employers to treat equal employment simply as a nuisance and not as something they were obligated to promote. Attempts by the Post Office to obtain more detailed and supplementary reports in addition to the forms required under Title VII of the Civil Rights Act ran into considerable industry opposition.

The Johnson Executive Order (No. 11246, September 24, 1965), which created a new agency, the Office of Federal Contract Compliance (OFCC) in place of the Kennedy President's Committee on Equal Employment Opportunity and placed OFCC within the Department of Labor, nevertheless continued most of the provisions of the second Kennedy order and the Post Office remained in charge of compliance in the trucking industry. Both the Post Office and the OFCC found that truckers were reluctant to alter their hiring practices and particularly feared making a change in the sleeper cab situation. It became very obvious that only government compulsion could effectuate a change. Fear of union opposition, of white worker resentment, and of being ostracized by management peers all contributed to the reluctance to change.

While the companies want to fall in line, an official says, they also want someone to blame for hiring Negroes. [A Post Office Department official said:] "We're willing to take the blame." "This way they can go to the country club and blame the damn government and escape any personal reaction by their friends. We've even had midnight conferences with employers at their request so other business men won't see what's going on." [78]

Top echelon Teamster officials were not making any public statements about government efforts to integrate the industry. It is not difficult to substantiate the employer's contention that local union leaders were antagonistic about hiring Negroes. The president of Teamsters' Local 100 in Cincinnati made public his sentiments when he said, "Would you like to climb into a bunk bed that a nigger just got out of?" [79] The president of Teamster Local 24, located in Akron, Ohio, declared, "To my knowledge, no law has been written yet that says a white has to bed down with Negroes." [80]

Admittedly, there were differences among employers and among local union officials as to the extent to which they would assist in promoting equal employment in the trucking industry. But the firms that realized they would eventually have to hire Negroes for the better-paying jobs were rare exceptions.

In 1967, one firm in the South hired two Negro road drivers to drive together in a sleeper cab operation. When one of the Negro drivers voluntarily quit, the company decided to place the remaining Negro road driver on what is referred to as the extra board. Normally, the men on this board are assigned on a first-in, first-out basis—depending, of course, on the volume and type of trucking services demanded on any particular day. When the Negro road driver reached the top of the list, the company, con-

---

78. "Bias Behind the Wheel," *Commercial Car Journal*, June 1966, p. 114.

79. *Wall Street Journal*, March 31, 1966.

80. *Ibid.*

trary to terms of the contract, simply bypassed him. As top man on the list, the Negro driver could have bid on a sleeper cab operation and chosen his partner. The company argued that it bypassed the Negro driver so as to avoid dismissing a white driver who might refuse to ride with him.

Although the company took the above action to avoid a direct confrontation with the local union, union officials attempted to solicit complaints from the white road drivers because the company had bypassed the Negro, and a grievance was filed and later withdrawn. The IBT's impetus was not that of protecting the Negro's rights, but actually was an attempt to make things so difficult for the company that it would discharge the Negro driver. Company spokesmen contend that the grievance was withdrawn because of pressure exerted by top echelon union officials who were pressured by some top government leaders.

While some companies apparently made some efforts to comply, others fought the government head on. One southern firm refused to desegregate its facilities. Other firms would agree to meet with the compliance examiner, but then would claim that the official the examiner was to talk with was sick or out of town when the government's representative arrived for the meeting. In many cases, local union leaders were less willing to meet with compliance examiners than were company officials.

In July 1967, Nagle was named by Postmaster General O'Brien to head the Equal Employment Opportunity Office within and for the Post Office Department. Nagle was committed to equal employment goals and communicated this spirit to his men in the field. The general impression was that Congressmen had started to receive complaints from white drivers and that Nagle was transferred to supervise a less sensitive activity.

Although Nagle resigned as Deputy Contract Compliance Officer in July 1967, a replacement was not named until February 1968. In the interim, the Department's contract compliance examiners continued to review the equal employment posture of new companies, or conducted follow-up reviews to determine the degree to which companies were implementing affirmative action programs. In addition, the examiners investigated cases of alleged discrimination arising because of individual complaints. Between July 1, 1967 and July 1, 1968 the Post Office Department processed approximately sixty such complaints. Should a firm refuse to make the necessary adjustments where discrimination was evident, the Department would hold informal hearings.

Hearings were also held when particular companies refused to demonstrate any intention of abiding by the provisions of Executive Order 11246. The Department conducted these informal hearings in Washington or if the companies refused to send representatives to Washington, at the companies' corporate headquarters. The industry soon discovered that it was better to send spokesmen to Washington because when examiners scheduled an informal hearing at a particular corporate location, they used this occasion to visit all the firms in the area. Much of the governments' activity was an exercise in futility, however. As one Department staff member put it, "During these informal hearings [the companies] said they were going to do something, but in fact they did nothing." [81]

In retrospect, the problem plaguing the Office of Federal Contract Compliance and the Post Office Department has remained the same over the years: the questionable nature of their authority to place companies found in violation on a proscribed list. The Department continued to threaten individual firms and the industry as a whole with debarment, but the industry was well aware that in the absence of legal precedents, the government was groping in the dark. No company in any industry has ever been debarred from contracts, perhaps because the penalty is so severe and the authority of the government to act remains uncertain.

THE POST OFFICE, THE OFCC, AND AFFIRMATIVE ACTION

Affirmative action is a nebulous term that means different things to different people. Government officials have never defined it precisely or legally, but Paul Nagle came close with his remarks on what was necessary to comply with the Presidential Executive Orders:

1. A company should have a declaration of policy.

2. The company should also have a person designated to administer that policy.

3. That person should also be designated to receive reports about how the various echelons of management are doing. The company should evaluate its operation to determine where it might be discriminating. For example, I've encountered some companies who had segregated

---

81. Personal interview, 1968.

washrooms without having been aware that they did have these washrooms at some terminals. We've also had the problem where the Negro local drivers had not been aule to get into over-the-road positions.

A broader aspect which I consider useful is. . .

4. Present employees should be evaluated from the standpoint of their potential to see whether they have been employed at a lower level than what they might be capable of doing. This should apply to applicants of any race to see whether they might have skills which are going untouched for some reason.

5. To provide training for persons who had previously been denied training opportunities granted to the majority of employees.

6. To advance a person who has been given this type of training if it's possible.

7. To make sure that the normal suppliers of personnel are aware that the company is not only stating a freedom from discrimination policy, but is actively pursuing it.

8. To make sure that seniority is used to aid rather than to hinder equal opportunity.

9. To have a fixed program of going out to determine what the community thinks of the particular company's pattern of behavior.

10. To go to schools in the vicinity to make sure the schools are aware of the affirmative action plan.

This is a comprehensive program and any combination of ten points is a limited category of affirmative action but taken together those points constitute a very forthright approach.[82]

Edward C. Sylvester, former director of the Office of Federal Contract Compliance, made it quite clear to the motor carriers that the government had no intention of defining affirmative action. Sylvester asserted that even if employers were to follow all the suggested steps issued by the POD, they still might not be operating in accordance with the Executive Order's intent. The very rationale of the order was to place the responsibility of affirmative action upon the employers' shoulders. Individual employers were expected to evaluate their potential hiring

---

82. Remarks of Paul A. Nagle, Deputy Contracts Compliance Officer, before American Trucking Associations' Industrial Relations Committee, San Francisco, California, November 15, 1965. A more detailed assessment of the Post Office Department's understanding of affirmative action is found in Appendix C.

needs and were to take any action they believed would augment the number of minorities on their payrolls. Once the employer did this, it was the government's task to determine whether the actions taken were "adequate and sufficient." [83]

Sylvester's contention that affirmative action will vary from one contractor to another, from one area to another, and even "from one day to the next," [84] reflects the breadth of the concept, but it left the industry in somewhat of a quandry. There virtually were as many opinions as to what constituted affirmative action as there were trucking firms contacted by the POD. While one employer maintained that the government was demanding that his firm hire Negroes in proportion to the number of Negroes living in a given area (quotas), another company representative believed the government was going to evaluate intent and not results per se.

One employer noted that at corporate headquarters his firm had approximately 100 people on the payroll. He claimed that the contract compliance examiner assigned to his company told him that there were 5.2 percent Negroes residing in the city, and that in ninety days the government expected to find the same percentage of Negroes employed by his company. It was, in the words of the employer, "just cut and dried." [85] The examiner even suggested that the company sponsor an open house of the company's facilities for Negroes. The firm refused to go this far, but it did put ads in the paper and it contacted a private employment agency in quest of Negro applicants. Yet no Negroes applied.

The second employer said that what the Post Office Department wanted the companies to do was "to go out and beat the bushes." [86] The government did not expect employers to hire unqualified people. What it did want the industry to do was to contact new employment sources which might be closer to the Negro labor supply. In fact, the Post Office Department had supplied his firm with Negro labor sources for twelve distinct terminal facilities.

A southern-domiciled firm questioned its obligation to contact minority groups. The firm's representative reported that their

---

83. *Applying Equal Employment in Trucking, Proceedings of the 16th Annual National Forum on Trucking Industrial Relations*, p. 18.

84. *Ibid.*

85. *Ibid.*, p. 188.

86. *Ibid.*, p. 189.

legal counsel even advised against it.[87] The rationale was that it had no idea of the leadership of these Negro groups; the implication was that they did not want to deal with any "radical" Negro groups.

Looming behind the scene of this discussion of affirmative action was the industry's concern about where they were to obtain Negro drivers and whether the latters' accident rate was greater than that among white drivers. We have already demonstrated that the Post Office Department has no trouble in obtaining qualified drivers for its own trucks. In addition, a representative from Greyhound Lines said that his company had no difficulty in finding qualified Negroes to drive buses. During their training period they had a higher dropout record, but upon completing the training program Negro bus drivers performed as well as white drivers.[88] As for the Negroes' accident experiences, the Greyhound representative said, ". . . I have yet to hear of one of them being involved in a serious accident." [89]

The motor carriers were told that taking affirmative action did not place them in a "Utopia Area." [90] The employer making this observation recounted how his firm had two Negro drivers—one with twenty-five years' experience and another with sixteen—who drove as a team. Pressure exerted by the Post Office Department caused the company to split these two drivers up and hire two more Negroes, but "still the pressure is being applied." [91]

One employer insisted that the government via its affirmative action doctrine was asking the industry to show the Negro preferential treatment. He objected to advertising in Negro papers because, "Then I'm going to have to advertise in a Jewish neighborhood newspaper, and an Irish, and a Polish" one.[92] Although this particular employer's criticism of affirmative action can be interpreted as somewhat extreme, the industry, in the summer of 1966, seemed more concerned with the technicalities of what to do to avoid government sanctions leveled against it than with the positive steps it should take to hire more Negroes.

---

87. *Ibid.*, p. 177.

88. *Ibid.*, p. 102.

89. *Ibid.*, p. 110.

90. *Ibid.*, p. 184.

91. *Ibid.*

92. *Ibid.*, p. 183.

Affirmative Action in Practice

Our own observation that the larger companies refused to change their hiring practices was supported by information obtained by another method from that employed in this study. In June 1968, the Post Office Department asked its compliance examiners to submit special reports detailing the breakthroughs that had been made by the companies for which they were responsible. In these reports the examiners enumerated the variables which they believed influenced the companies in their less-than-enthusiastic response to equal employment opportunities hiring procedures and goals. Below is a brief summary from the reports submitted by seventeen of the Department's examiners.

The examiners acknowledged that without meaningful affirmative action programs employers would be virtually unable to increase the number of Negroes on their payrolls. First, the present hiring procedures—pirating from other firms, informal referral systems, and reliance upon union hiring halls—were employment streams in which Negroes were unlikely to be found. Second, Negroes are reluctant (even when aware of openings and qualified) to seek employment in hostile environments. Finally, most of the companies found in the motor carrier industry lacked the administrative talent necessary for the implementation of successful equal employment opportunities programs.

Against this background, not a single firm, according to the contract compliance examiners, had made any breakthroughs.[93] Employers were simply complacent. Although some companies did make slight advances in employing Negroes, the net result was mere tokenism. In general, the examiner discovered that a few companies were hiring more Negroes, even as road drivers, but only at one or two terminal facilities. Discrimination prevailed throughout the industry, according to the examiners, because management did not realize fully what compliance meant, or because of duplicity and insincerity in their dealing with the government, or a combination of these. It was estimated that less than 15 percent of all Class I motor carriers had taken the minimal first step—writing an affirmative action program. Companies have been reluctant, furthermore, to view training programs as a means of enhancing an affirmative action program, even when drivers were in short supply.

---

93. Information based on interviews, 1968.

Later Developments and Progress

In February 1968, Clarence H. Featherson, former EEOC field investigator, was named Deputy Contract Compliance Officer, the position vacated by Nagle in June 1967. The Post Office compliance staff was expanded, and the Post Office Department inaugurated a special review program designed to gather more precise information about the equal employment practices of a representative group of nineteen of the nation's larger carriers. Such information could provide the basis for "pattern of discrimination" cases filed by the U.S. Department of Justice pursuant to Title VII of the Civil Rights Act, as will be discussed later in this chapter. The decision of the courts in the cases involving discriminatory seniority systems in the tobacco [94] and paper [95] industries provided possible clues to action in other industries, such as trucking, where management and union policies were adversely affecting Negro job opportunities.

With this objective in mind, examiners assigned to these nineteen trucking companies were instructed to: (1) take an inventory of all employees by job category, indicating race and national origin; (2) identify persons on the seniority rosters by race; (3) list new hires for the preceding six months by race and job categories; (4) obtain a copy of the company's equal employment policy statement; (5) obtain copies of letters sent to referral sources stating the company's equal employment opportunity commitment; (6) obtain copies of current collective bargaining agreements; (7) obtain a current list of qualifications for job categories; and (8) obtain samples of tests administered to job applicants.

The examiners were also requested to: (1) interview minority employees to determine what is actually occurring with regard to hiring, promotion, transfer, training, etc., and (2) interview community organizations to determine the extent to which the contractor has communicated with minority referral sources, specifically: (a) the nature of such contact—whether oral or written; (b) the content of such contact, i.e., whether actual job referrals have been solicited or whether contact has consisted only of statements of philosophy; and (c) the consequences of

---

94. *Quarles* v. *Philip Morris, Inc.*, 279 F Supp. 505 (E.D. Va. 1968).

95. *United States* v. *Local 189, United Papermakers and Paperworkers, et al.*, 282 F Supp. 39 (E.D. La., 1968); affirmed, —— F. 2d —— (5th Cir., 1969).

such contact: whether referrals have been made to the company and what the results of such referrals may have been.

Table 31 shows the number of Negroes these nineteen companies had on their payrolls prior to January 1968, and the number of Negroes employed during the first six months of 1968. During this period the total number of Negroes employed by the nineteen companies increased slightly from 2,171 to 2,509. The proportion of Negroes among the total number of people employed increased from 4.0 percent to 4.3 percent.

Since 1965, the Post Office Department has concentrated its affirmative action drive on the over-the-road driver job classification. The nineteen companies increased the number of Negro road drivers from 62 out of a total of 9,168 to 98 out of a total of 9,845. Although this is admittedly a nearly 60 percent increase in the number of Negro drivers, from January to June 1968, it represents only a miniscule percentage increase from 0.7 to 1.0 percent of the drivers employed.

Negroes made their greatest advance in the operatives category as city drivers. Of the 227 city drivers hired in the six-month period, 42 or 18.5 percent were Negroes. Should this trend continue, it is possible that more Negroes, having gained acceptance as city drivers, will eventually be employed as road drivers.

The first half 1968 new hire data, as shown in Table 31, are indicative of Negro manpower utilization for the nation at large and do not reflect the degree to which particular labor markets have supplied blacks to the trucking industry. A government spokesman maintained, however, "that the most encouraging minority utilization did not come from the Northern or Western cities, but instead from two Southern-domiciled corporations." [96] In turn, these two southern firms employed 90 percent of the Negro drivers and 25 percent of the minority office and clerical employees.

The continued absence of Negroes in white collar jobs, and why relatively few companies responded to the government's request to establish effective affirmative action programs is explained, according to a government spokesman, by two factors. First, although most companies have established what they con-

---

96. Remarks made by Clarence H. Featherson, the Post Office Department's deputy contract compliance officer. These comments appeared in *Trucking Labor Relations Information*, Vol. 23, Sec. 4, No. 33, November 15, 1968 (Washington: American Trucking Associations), p. 2.

TABLE 31. Trucking Industry
Total Employees and New Hires by Race
19 Class I Carriers, January 1 to June 30, 1968

Job Categories	Prior and New Hires			Prior Employment			New Hires			Difference—Present and Former Per-cent Negro
	Total	Total Negro	Percent Negro	Total	Total Negro	Percent Negro	Total	Total Negro	Percent Negro	
Officials-Managers	4,748	20	0.4	4,475	11	0.2	273	9	3.3	+0.2
Professionals	250	5	2.0	239	4	1.7	11	1	9.1	+0.3
Technicians	113	4	3.5	90	2	2.2	23	2	8.7	+1.3
Sales workers	1,313	1	0.1	1,223	—	—	90	1	1.1	+0.1
Office-clerical	8,684	219	2.5	7,641	130	1.7	1,043	89	8.5	+0.8
Craftsmen	3,797	126	3.3	3,523	98	2.8	274	28	10.2	+0.5
Operatives										
Road drivers	9,845	98	1.0	9,168	62	0.7	677	36	5.3	+0.3
City drivers	4,850	328	6.8	4,623	286	6.2	227	42	18.5	+0.5
Dockmen	3,974	332	8.4	3,574	275	7.7	400	57	14.3	+0.7
Others	16,690	1,006	6.0	16,133	997	6.2	557	9	1.6	-0.2
Laborers (Unskilled)	3,349	257	7.7	3,110	210	6.8	239	47	19.7	+0.9
Service workers	465	113	24.3	424	96	22.6	41	17	41.5	+1.7
Total	58,078	2,509	4.3	54,223	2,171	4.0	3,855	338	8.8	+0.3

Source: U.S. Post Office.

sider to be worthwhile affirmative action programs, these corporate endeavors had effectuated little change in practice. Second, comprehensive minority employment plans were often formulated at the corporate level, but there was a communication breakdown between headquarters and the companies' many terminals.[97]

Throughout 1969 the Post Office Department not only continued to conduct compliance reviews at the corporate and terminal levels, but it also started to stress the necessity of companies cooperating in the development of training programs. These governmental efforts at promoting training and the industry's response to this will be discussed in some detail later in this chapter. Table 32, however, shows how many Negroes were new hires during the first six months of 1969 and also the jobs in which they were hired. These recent new-hire trends are a consequence of the federal government's continued prodding of the industry and not primarily a result of training programs.

TABLE 32. *Trucking Industry*
New Hires by Race and Occupational Group
358 Trucking Companies, January 1 to June 30, 1969

Occupational Groups	New Hires		
	Total	Negro	Percent Negro
Officials and managers	1,186	15	1.3
Professionals	15	—	—
Technicians	429	6	1.4
Sales workers	410	4	1.0
Office and clerical	5,804	251	4.3
Total white collar	7,844	276	3.5
Craftsmen	1,270	128	10.1
Operatives			
Road drivers	5,589	567	10.1
City drivers	5,711	573	10.0
Dockmen	5,348	1,078	20.1
Others	40	7	17.5
Laborers	789	195	24.7
Service workers	451	125	27.7
Total blue collar	19,198	2,673	13.9
Total	27,042	2,949	10.9

Source: U.S. Post Office Department.

97. *Ibid.*

The 358 firms from which the first-half 1969 statistics were obtained, employed in 1968 a total of 231,325 people, of which 17,794 [98] or 7.7 percent were minority employees. Although this minority classification included American Indians and Spanish-speaking workers in addition to Negroes, it should be noted that during the first six months of 1969 2,949 or 10.9 percent of the 27,042 new hires were Negroes. Because the 1968 new hire statistics, as shown in Table 31, represent the employment results of nineteen Class I motor carriers, while the 1969 data are representative of the hiring activities of 358 trucking companies, it is difficult to infer the precise significance of these yearly differences. Yet, it does seem that Negroes are making some gains in some of the better-paying job classifications included under the blue collar category. For example, 10.1 percent of all road drivers hired in 1969 were Negroes. Even when we allow for the different sources of statistics for 1968 and 1969, the trend is upward when we consider the fact that only 5.3 percent of the road drivers hired by the nineteen Class I carriers in 1968 were Negroes.

Training as Affirmative Action

In recent years the larger carriers have debated openly the necessity of the industry's promoting coordinated driver training programs. Although some state trucking associations have sponsored intermittent driver training schools and the American Trucking Associations [99] has investigated the feasibility of such programs, the net effect of these efforts has been rather insignificant. Funding, control, and screening are several of the basic fundamentals over which disagreement within the industry abounds. Because various types of carriers necessarily insist upon diverse skill requirements for their drivers, it is difficult to develop a comprehensive program capable of satisfying the divergent needs of all. Consequently, the industry has been reluctant to promote or sponsor training programs, even in a tight labor situation when competent drivers are hard to find. The subsequent presentation pertaining to the employers' attitudes toward training programs must be viewed against this background of past inertia and failures in respect to such programs.

---

98. Data in author's possession.

99. For a discussion of some of the obstacles presented in establishing and implementing training programs, see *Training in the Trucking Industry* (Washington: American Trucking Associations, 1963).

The possibilities of affirmative action would seem to be great. Of the 111 firms interviewed, 88, or 79 percent, acknowledged that they were unable to find sufficient skilled drivers. Of these 88 firms, 34 percent said that this shortage of drivers was confined to the over-the-road job classification. Another 9 percent of the firms maintained that their difficulty was in finding local drivers, and 57 percent contended that they were short of both local and over-the-road drivers. In turn, of the 88 firms, 84 percent reported that the shortage of drivers was system-wide, while the remaining 16 percent said it was confined to specific labor markets. (The variation in the labor markets noted was so great that it was not possible to discern any pattern of labor shortage in specific areas of the nation.)

Private truck driver training schools are located throughout the nation, usually near the large urban centers where a great number of terminals are located. The tuition, which is usually paid by the trainee, can range from $500 to $800. Sixty-six, or 59 percent of the companies interviewed, knew of existing private schools in the areas where they maintained terminals, but only 23 companies, or 21 percent, had ever hired drivers who had graduated from these schools. Companies that did hire these drivers were not satisfied with their driving ability and, consequently, the company had to give further on-the-job training. Driving hazards and conditions are nearly impossible to simulate and the schools do not enable their trainees to cope with the psychological pressures associated with driving a truck day in and day out. Some employers contended that these private schools often accepted candidates who lacked even the basic qualifications, and engaged in misleading advertising campaigns. It would be well beyond the scope of this study to evaluate driver training programs, but note should be taken that some advances have been made in programs under federal auspices.

For the most part, larger carriers also are reluctant to establish their own training programs because of the expense entailed and because pirating employees is a common practice among firms in the industry. Seven of the 111 firms interviewed underwrite their own driver training schools, but only three of these are conducted on a permanent basis and they can serve only a few labor markets.

In raising questions related to training, the author was not interested in training as such, but rather sought to determine whether the employers, without prompting, would admit to a direct correlation between formal training and the affirmative action mandate embodied in Executive Order 11246. Only three representatives of the companies interviewed took the lead and implied that this should be the route followed by the industry if it seriously desired to meet the government's mandate. This indicates that the industry as a whole does not intend to provide training as an important and constructive avenue of affirmative action.

In early 1969, the Post Office Department shifted its emphasis from conducting compliance reviews to developing comprehensive manpower training programs. The government probably concluded that compliance reviews, usually conducted every ninety days, were no longer having a significant impact upon the hiring of Negroes in the better-paying jobs. Therefore, in an effort to encourage a fuller utilization of Negro manpower, and in particular, black over-the-road drivers, the Post Office Department began stressing the importance of training programs as an integral ingredient of the Executive Order's affirmative action provision. Coupled with this emphasis on training was the government's insistence that employers validate screening procedures used in hiring.

Rather than develop a comprehensive national model for these training programs, the Post Office Department directed its compliance examiners in the field to try to obtain the cooperation of the Teamsters, state trucking associations, individual employers, and community groups in twenty distinct labor markets. The responses of the industry and the Teamsters have been mixed. Some companies have released instructors and supervisory personnel to help develop these training programs, but this is the exception and certainly not reflective of the industry in general. Most companies, moreover, are unwilling to guarantee that they will hire any of those completing these proposed training programs.

Early in 1969 the government expressed an intention to establish training centers in twenty major labor markets, but as of the early months of 1970, only six programs had begun. Of these six embryonic programs, only the one proposed in Cleveland had a reasonable degree of employer support, and even this one is not likely to be in operation until mid-1970.

The employer's less-than-enthusiastic response to the government's overtures requesting their cooperation in the area of training must be viewed against a background of the industry's historic attitude toward training programs. Before equal employment was even a factor in employment practices, trucking companies were reluctant to participate in multiemployer training programs. Even though the majority of employers contend that they cannot find qualified applicants, they know that as wages increase among public carriers they will be able to continue to pirate—especially drivers—from the private carriers.

Sanctions under the Executive Order

The only sanction under the Executive Order is debarment from doing business with the government. This has never been used against the trucking or any other industry, probably for two reasons. First, it is too strong a penalty, involving as it does for most industries loss of business not only with the government, but with all concerns doing business with the government as well. The net effect is most likely forced cessation of business and unemployment for those employed—an action not likely to be without broad political, as well as economic, repercussions.

Second, there is a very real legal question of the propriety of what is, without doubt, executive law making which must restrain even the most activist among the federal officials in the civil rights field. For example, in early 1967, the Post Office Department forwarded the case histories of four of the more recalcitrant trucking companies to the OFCC, and requested that this latter agency apply sanctions against these companies. The OFCC returned these cases to the Department, claiming that the information was inadequate. The Department resubmitted these cases in mid-1967, but at the time of this writing action is still pending. One can well imagine the hesitation of the government to open the Pandora's box involved with court perusal of the legality (and meaning) of affirmative action, for example, or even of the right of the Executive to issue orders going beyond the terms of what Congress has already legislated. It is perhaps for this reason that enforcement proceedings pursuant to the Civil Rights Act of 1964 have been preferred by the Department of Justice and other government officials, rather than hazarding action pursuant to an Executive Order.[100] The following section discusses such cases.

---

100. The Executive Order has been included in some legal proceedings, but the key thrust has been pursuant to Title VII of the 1964 law.

COURT PROCEEDINGS

The lack of progress in equal employment in the trucking industry led to a number of court cases, filed both by individual complainants after the Equal Employment Opportunity Commission had failed to resolve the issue by conciliation, and by the Department of Justice, pursuant to Section 707 of the Civil Rights Act of 1964. Under this law, the Attorney General has the authority to sue whenever he

. . . has reasonable cause to believe that any person or group of persons is engaged in a pattern or practice of resistance to the full enjoyment of any of the rights secured by this title, and that the pattern or practice is of such a nature and is intended to deny the full exercise of the rights herein described.[101]

A brief review of the key court cases, and their status as of December 1969, points up further the civil rights problems in the industry. The precise sequence of events are enumerated in the first case only, but the basic procedure for cases filed by individuals in the remaining cases are similar.

Richard Johnson, Jr. v. Georgia Highway Express [102]

Georgia Highway Express is a general freight carrier headquartered in Atlanta, maintaining approximately thirty terminal facilities throughout Georgia, Alabama, and Tennessee. The complainant contended that he was discharged from the terminal in Atlanta because of his civil rights activities.

In February 1966, the man allegedly discriminated against attended a meeting at the Atlanta facility attended by some of his Negro coworkers. Acting as spokesman for the group, he asked the company representatives present at the meeting what the firm intended to do about equal employment. In particular, the Negro spokesman noted the equal employment posters and asked when Negroes would be permitted to apply for jobs other than that of dockmen—especially road driver positions. Although the complainant had worked for the company since August 1961, he was discharged on March 22, 1966.

---

101. The Civil Rights Act of 1964, Section 707(a).

102. *Richard Johnson, Jr.* v. *Georgia Highway Express*, C.A. No. 11.598 (N.D. Ga.) 59 L.C. 9193 (October 8, 1968).

All the Negroes employed at this particular terminal are dock-men. As a result of the meeting, three Negroes were promoted to supervisory positions on the docks, but none were given jobs as drivers. During the past fifteen years, the company continually promoted white dockmen to the position of city driver, but this line of progression was not open to Negroes. This practice persisted even though over 90 percent of the dock workers were Negroes.

On March 31, 1966, within ninety days of his discharge (this ninety-day period was stipulated in Title VII at that time) the complainant filed his case with the EEOC. Sixteen months later, in July 1967, the Commission notified the aggrieved party that within the meaning of Title VII, it had reasonable cause to believe that the company had committed an unlawful practice. The Commission, after failing to eliminate said practice by conciliation, notified the complainant on January 29, 1968 that he was entitled to seek relief through civil action before the federal district court.

Seeking adequate relief, the lawyers for the plaintiff requested the court to issue a private and permanent injunction against Georgia Highway Express, and to compel the company to give the plaintiff back pay to compensate for the loss of income he suffered as a result of the discharge. In addition, the plaintiff also sought to protect all people of his class by forcing the company to hire Negroes as local and road drivers.

The company argued that the court lacked jurisdiction because as a discharged employee the plaintiff no longer represented the interest of the firm's employees. The company also contended that the aggrieved party was discharged because of his high rate of tardiness and absenteeism. The defendant, in turn, argued that the Attorney General can prosecute a company whenever he "has reasonable cause to believe that any person or group of persons is engaged in a pattern and practice of resistance." [103] Inasmuch as the Attorney General failed to take such action, the defendant argued that it was not in fact engaged in a "pattern and practice" of discrimination as the lawyers for the plaintiff implied. Georgia Highway Express requested, moreover, that there should be trial by jury.

The U.S. District Court ruled in June 1968 that the injunction would be denied because the plaintiff could not process this case as a class action. The lawyers for the plaintiff filed a motion to

103. *Ibid.*

permit an interlocutary appeal because the status of class actions
in a civil rights case was a controlling question of law about
which there is substantial ground for a difference of opinion.
The judge in the case conceded that a true question of law existed and granted the plaintiff the right of appeal.

The case was appealed, and on October 30, 1969 the United
States Court of Appeals (Fifth Circuit) handed down a decision
in favor of the plaintiff. The District Court had restricted the
scope of the class the plaintiff could represent to those persons
who had been discharged because of their race. Upon appeal,
however, the higher court acknowledged that the appellant's suit
was an " 'across the board' attack on unequal employment practices alleged to have been committed by the appellee pursuant to
its policy of racial discrimination," [104] and that he could represent applicants, as well as Negroes who may have been discharged. In upholding the plaintiff's right to sue for all Negroes
in a class action, the court referred to a former school desegre-
gation case which stated:

> The peculiar rights of specific individuals were not in controversy. It
> [the suit] was directed at the system wide policy of racial discrimination.
> It sought obliteration of that policy of system wide racial discrimination.
> In various ways this was sought through suitable declaratory orders and
> injunctions against any rule, regulation, custom or practice having any
> such consequence. *Potts* v. *Flax*, 5 Cir. 1963, 313 F.2d 284, 289.[105]

As for the trial by jury which was requested by the company,
this likewise was denied the defendant. In arguing that the only
issue was a claim for back pay, the company contended that this
should be decided by a trial jury. The circuit court, in denying
the defendant his request for trial by jury, held that only after
the case had been heard on a class action could the court decide
if the plaintiff had de facto been discriminated against. In turn,
if the fact of discrimination is established in future litigation, it
will be the court's obligation to decide the back pay issue.

As of January 1970, the lawyers for the plaintiff were still
engaged in pretrial discovery procedures. In some of these racial
employment discovery procedures employers are often requested
to supply answers and evidence to as many as 250 posed ques-

---

104. *Richard Johnson, Jr.* v. *Georgia Highway Express, Inc.*, C.A. No. 11.598
     (N.D. Ga. 1968) 59 L.C. 9193; reversed and remanded —— F. 2d ——
     (5th Cir., 1969).

105. *Idem.*

tions. It is estimated that a case of this nature can take any-
where from three months to a year before it is scheduled and
the class action allegation is ultimately decided by the court. It
is well to recall that the plaintiff's initial complaint to the Equal
Employment Opportunity Commission was submitted in March
1966.

Lee v. Observer Transportation [106]

This case involves a nonunion trucker located in Charlotte,
North Carolina. Eighteen Negroes filed a charge against this firm
because of alleged lower wages paid Negroes. They alleged that
Negro drivers received $1.50 per hour, while white drivers were
being paid $1.79 per hour. The complainants also contended that
they were refused the better-paying road jobs.

Of the forty-eight local drivers, only seven are white and five
of these were promoted subsequent to the filing of the original
complaint. There were twenty-five dock workers employed at this
terminal, but only two of them were white and these were hired
after the complaint was lodged against the company. It seems
that the company found it more expedient to integrate the lower
range of the job hierarchy by hiring a few whites than it did
to hire Negroes as road drivers. Again, the sole Negro road
driver was promoted to this job after the complaint was submitted.

The EEOC investigated the case and subsequently notified the
complainants that they would have to go to court to receive adequate relief. When the case went to court, the lawyers for the
defendant did not even address themselves to the substantive
matter of allegations, but rather argued that the court lacked
jurisdiction. The firm's contention was that the EEOC had
made no attempt whatsoever to eliminate the alleged discrimination by mediation or other informal methods. This, they argued,
was a necessary prerequisite before the filing of a formal suit.

The lawyers for the plaintiff requested that the court grant
a preliminary and permanent injunction enjoining the defendant
from the alleged practices and from interfering with the plaintiff's rights. The plaintiff was also requesting back pay from the
time of his alleged wrongful denial of equal employment opportunities. In denying these requests, the U.S. District Court, on

---

106. *Lee* v. *Observer Transportation*, C.A. No. 2145 (W.D.N.C.), dismissed
59 L.C. 9206, reversed by the Fourth Circuit Court of Appeals, 59 L.C.
9207, cert. denied by the Supreme Court on March 24, 1969.

January 25, 1968, ruled that conciliation was in fact a prerequisite to the plaintiff's right to file or maintain a civil action under Section 703 of the Civil Rights Act of 1964.

Upon appeal, however, the U.S. Circuit Court of Appeals for the Fourth Circuit reversed the decision of the Circuit Court when it held that conciliation per se was not a prerequisite to the plaintiff's right of civil action. The defendant appealed this decision to the U.S. Supreme Court, but the latter refused to hear the case. As of January 1970, the substantive issues of the case were being investigated by the lawyers of the plaintiff through discovery procedures.

Hairston v. McLean Trucking Company [107]

With its headquarters located in the Winston-Salem, North Carolina area, McLean Trucking has over 5,000 employees on its payrolls and sixty-five terminals located in twenty states. This complaint of alleged discrimination was filed by a Negro employed by the firm's wholly-owned subsidiary, Modern Automotive Services, Inc., which provides automotive services at the parent company's headquarters.

The complainant, a maintenance man in the tire department of the subsidiary company, maintained that the employer uses a hiring and promotion system which tends to exclude Negroes from the better-paying jobs. There were no Negroes in the body, paint, trailer, automotive, or parts department. Aside from the management and clerical personnel working at the corporate headquarters, the Winston-Salem terminal has essentially three groups of employees: over-the-road drivers, local drivers, and maintenance men. Both categories of drivers are employed by the parent firm, while the maintenance men, although working at the same location, are employed by the subsidiary company. In turn, the Teamsters' local in the area is party to three distinct labor agreements: two with the parent company for local and over-the-road drivers respectively, and one with the subsidiary maintenance company.

Because the subsidiary company has a departmental seniority system, any Negro transferring to a different department would lose his seniority, and the complainant contends that this promotional system deprives him of opportunities for advancement. But

---

107. *Hairston* v. *McLean Trucking Company,* C.A. No. C-77-WS-68, (U.S.D.C., W.D.N.C.).

the firm's promotional policy in fact does not allow a man to transfer from one job classification to another, nor does it permit an employee to resign from one job and then reapply for another. When this policy is combined with the practice of hiring Negroes only as tiremen, minority members are locked into a dead end department (tire department) where promotional opportunities are nonexistent. The charging party, a member of this department, requested to be admitted to the company's driver training program.

The employer held that because the complainant is an employee of Modern Automotive Services, Inc. a charge against the McLean Trucking Company is not appropriate. Although the parent company negotiates the labor contracts of the subsidiary firm, and formulates and implements its hiring and upgrading policies, it argues that it should not be party to the case.

The defendant also argued that even if the charging party had been white, his request for a transfer would have been denied. While this contention might be true, there are no whites isolated in the lowest-paying jobs offered by either the parent or subsidiary companies. Moreover, virtually all the Negroes employed by both the companies are locked in these non-status, low-paying, dead end job categories.

McLean Trucking refused to answer some of the questions submitted by the lawyers for the plaintiff on the grounds that these questions were irrelevant and immaterial to the case at hand. For example, the defendant objected to having to provide the address of the company that hires employees for its subsidiary, Modern Automotive Services, Inc., which provides maintenance service for McLean's fleet. On November 12, 1968, the plaintiff asked the court to compel the company to answer all the questions submitted in the interrogation or discovery procedures. McLean countered this move by filing a motion requesting that the court deny the plaintiff the right to answer any and all questions he might submit. As of January 1970 neither the plaintiff's nor the defendant's requests had been decided by the courts.

James v. Braswell Motor [108]

This complaint, lodged against a southern terminal in Dallas, Texas was, unlike the former cases, the first claim under Title

---

108. *James* v. *Braswell Motor*, C.A. No. 3-2113 (N.D. Tex., May 1, 1968.)

VII involving any industry where the case was presented to a jury. The plaintiff asserted that Braswell Motor refused to promote him from the job of dockman to that of checker, despite its promise to do so. He further alleged that he was bypassed several times when the defendant promoted newly-hired white employees to the position of checker. This action on the part of the defendant was discriminatory, according to Title VII of the Civil Rights Act of 1964.

Inasmuch as dockmen were paid less than checkers, the plaintiff requested that the company pay him the difference in wages occasioned by this unlawful employment practice. The plaintiff also requested that the jury order the defendant to pay the fees of his attorney at the rate of $50.00 per hour. Although the defendant denied the allegations, the jury awarded the aggrieved Negro $1,800, plus six percent interest, which represented the difference in pay he would have received had he been promoted to the position of checker. The defendant was further ordered to pay the plaintiff's lawyer fee of $750.00.

The defendant's motion for a new trial asserted that the court erred in requiring the jury to make its determination on inadequate facts. Moreover, the court allegedly erred because Title VII only permits back pay for lost wages and not because a man was not promoted. The defendant requested that the court order a stay of any proceedings to enforce the judgment entered in favor of the plaintiff, pending the defendant's motion for a new trial. Like the cases noted above, this one is waiting a final verdict.

The above cases are prototypes of alleged claims of discrimination lodged against four distinct trucking companies. While the firms involved were different, the cases themselves manifest certain similar characteristics:

1. All the complaints arose because of hiring or upgrading practices pursued by terminals located in the South.

2. Although one of them was initially filed with the EEOC as early as September 1965, all of these cases are still being litigated.

3. In all the cases the defendants have questioned procedural questions of law, besides the factual data submitted by the aggrieved.

Bradshaw v. Associated Transport, Inc., and United States v. Associated Transport [109]

Associated Transport employs some 8,000 people throughout its operations, but these complaints arose when two Negroes sought employment at its Burlington, North Carolina terminal. The total number of people employed at this location was approximately 530, of which 200 were road drivers, but there were no Negroes in this latter job classification. Two distinct complaints were filed simultaneously, but only one of them is unique enough for a detailed discussion.

The Negro filing this particular complaint alleged that he was denied employment as a road driver because he failed to meet the two-year experience standard stipulated by Associated. When he told the party who conducted the interview that he was willing to pay his own tuition and attend the North Carolina Driving School in Raleigh, he was told that the company's policy was not to employ drivers graduated by this school.

Although the original complaint was filed in September 1965, the case is still pending. The defendant is not questioning the allegation made by the complainant that the company's employment standards were different for Negroes, but rather is arguing that the court lacks jurisdiction because the case was not presented to the federal district courts within the time span allowed under Title VII. Again the plaintiff is confronted with substantiating a point of law, and as yet has not been able to raise the question of the presence of discrimination.

On August 6, 1968, the Department of Justice filed a suit independent of the individual complaint and alleged that Associated Transport was guilty of perpetuating a "pattern and practice" of discrimination. With two distinct charges lodged against the company, the courts ordered the lawyers for Bradshaw (the original plaintiff) and the Department of Justice to consolidate their investigating activities. On May 14, 1969, however, the Department of Justice arrived at a conciliated agreement with Associated Transport. The original case which arose because of a singular alleged claim of discrimination is still pending.

---

109. *Bradshaw* v. *Associated Transport, Inc.,* C.A. No. C-245-G-67 (U.S.D.C., E.D.N.C.) ;*United States* v. *Associated Transport,* C.A. No. C-99-G-68 (U.S.D.C., E.D.N.C.).

United States v. Roadway Express [110]

After receiving nineteen complaints of alleged discrimination, the EEOC requested the Department of Justice to take action against Roadway Express, the fourth largest and one of the more profitable trucking companies in the nation. Roadway, with corporate offices in Akron, Ohio, operates in twenty-four states.

Among its approximate 9,000 employees Roadway employed only 288 Negroes, the EEOC discovered, and no Negroes were found among its 2,100 road drivers or its 1,300 managers, professionals, and sales workers. Of Roadway's 1,043 office and clerical employees, only two were Negroes. The remaining 286 Negroes were employed as garage workers, dock workers, pickup and delivery drivers, checkers, and service workers.

This case is unique in that it marked the first time the federal government brought suit against a company's nationwide operations, rather than a single plant or facility. With the Negro-white employment profile established, the Justice Department claimed that Roadway "pursued and continues to pursue policies and practices that discriminate against Negroes and which deprive them of employment opportunities or adversely affect their status as employees because of race." [111] In implementing these policies and practices Roadway was accused of: (1) failing or refusing to hire Negroes on the same basis as whites; (2) always assigning Negroes to the lower-paying jobs; (3) perpetuating separate lines of progression based on race; and (4) refusing to promote Negroes according to the same criteria used for white employees.

The suit seeks an injunction to end discrimination and requests that Roadway be compelled to take the necessary steps to modify its practices so that Negroes will be treated equitably. As are all the other cases noted above, this one is still in litigation. Because of the size of the firm and the scope of the case, this will no doubt set precedents for other civil rights cases in the area of employment.

---

110. *United States* v. *Roadway Express*, C.A. No. C-68-321 (U.S.D.C. N.D. Ohio).

111. *United States* v. *Roadway Express*, C.A. No. C-68-321 (U.S.D.C. N.D. Ohio).

*United States v. Central Motor Lines, Inc. and Locals 71, 391,
and 710, International Brotherhood of Teamsters* [112]

Central Motor Lines employs in the neighborhood of 1,500
people throughout its system and operates terminals in at least
eight states. The Department of Justice claims that the company
employs 73 Negroes and 544 whites at its Charlotte terminal,
and 25 Negroes and 63 whites at its Greensboro location. Of
greater significance is the fact that Central employs no Negroes
among its some 300 over-the-road drivers and only two Negroes
are local drivers among the 76 such employees working at the
Charlotte and Greensboro terminals.

Similar to the Roadway case, the federal government argued
that Central Motor Lines has failed to take adequate affirmative
steps to correct the continuing effects of discriminatory practices
and, therefore, this constituted a "pattern and practice" of resistance to the full utilization of Negroes. In this case, however,
the Attorney General also filed suit against three Teamster locals, namely, Local 71, Charlotte, N.C.; Local 391, Greensboro,
N.C.; and Local 710, Chicago, Illinois. The charge against the
Teamsters contends that the collective bargaining agreement with
Central Motor Lines contributes to the perpetuation of racial discrimination. Since the contract provides for seniority determination on the basis of separate job classifications (separate lists for
local and long-haul drivers) rather than length of service at a
particular terminal, Negroes—so claims the Department of Justice—are not promoted to over-the-road jobs. In a decision handed down by the United States Court of Appeals for the Fourth
Circuit, it has been decided that total service at a location, regardless of time on a job, should determine who is promoted
provided the employee has the ability to perform the job. [113] The
complexity of the Central case and past experience suggests that
it will take several years of litigation before it can be determined
whether the rationale of the above [114] case applies here.

Against this background of protracted litigation over the application of Title VII, in particular cases the trucking industry

---

112. *U.S.* v. *Central Motor Lines, Inc. and Locals 71, 391 and 710, International Brotherhood of Teamsters*, as reported in *Daily Labor Report*,
August 13, 1969.

113. *United States* v. *Local 189, United Papermakers and Paperworkers, et al.*,
282 F Supp. 39 (E.D. La. 1968); affirmed, —— F 2d —— (5th Cir.,
1969).

114. *Ibid.*

has been urged continuously by the Post Office Department to hire more Negroes. The industry is aware, however, that Title VII, although subject to judicial interpretation, might well prove to be the strongest antidiscrimination weapon at the government's disposal. The NAACP's Legal Defense and Education Fund, which usually represents the plaintiffs in Title VII cases, is aware that a whole body of decisions is necessary before the government can expedite any civil action that must be taken against discriminating employers. Until this happens, it is unlikely that the trucking industry will change its past practices and hire more Negroes, unless the government exercises its authority under Executive Order 11246 and prosecutes companies found in violation of the Order.

In May 1968, a trucking firm, namely B and P Motor Express of Pittsburgh, Pennsylvania, was one of five companies formally notified by the OFCC that the latter was contemplating barring them from government work. These companies, if they failed to request formal hearings, were to be declared automatically ineligible for further contracts and any existing contracts could be terminated. Although this is the first such instance of such notice, the OFCC has stepped up its practice of conducting informal conferences with representatives from individual trucking companies. It seems that the OFCC has decided that conciliation and persuasion have not convinced the industry as a whole of its obligation to hire Negroes in the better-paying job classifications. It is too early to tell whether OFCC's increased use of informal private conferences will be sufficient or whether formal methods will be necessary before truckers alter their employment practices.

ADMINISTRATIVE PROBLEMS IN CIVIL RIGHTS ENFORCEMENT

The progress toward equal employment opportunity in the industry, according to industry spokesmen, has been hindered by the jurisdictional overlap of the OFCC and the Post Office Department with the Equal Employment Opportunity Commission, which was created under Title VII of the Civil Rights Act of 1964. Generally, the industry preferred the Post Office inspectors because it found that Department's compliance examiners reasonable in their requests when they conducted investigations at the various firms' headquarters or terminal facilities. Most truckers found them much more understanding than the staff personnel of the EEOC. One company representative attributed this fundamental difference in attitude and approach to the fact that most of the compliance examiners employed by the Department were former officials of the United Federation of Postal Clerks. Nagle had been administrative vice president of this union and recruited his staff from among its ranks. Their previous experience in dealing with people, the company representative claimed, made them more sensitive to the numerous human problems arising when a firm attempts to integrate its work force.[115]

The industry's initial impression of the Department's compliance examiners still prevails. When the author questioned representatives of the interviewed sample firms about the ability, understanding, and attitude of the Department's compliance examiners, the general response was: "They have a job to do and they are doing it." From the employer's point of view, in 1968 only one compliance examiner seemed to be making unreasonable demands of them at specific terminal locations. Incidentally, when the author mentioned this to the Department's Washington staff, he was told that this particular examiner was as effective as the others in encouraging employers to hire more Negroes.

The industry found the Equal Employment Opportunity Commission's examiners much more aggressive and less understanding of their problems. Having come from other agencies, these investigators, as one employer stated, want "the letter of the law upheld regardless." [116] Unlike the Post Office Department, the EEOC was not interested in the spirit of the law. This same employer contended that the EEOC examiner usually "wants to know nothing from anything about conciliation." [117]

Not only were the truckers censorious of the contradictory differences in attitude and approach between the EEOC and the Department, but they soon had reason to criticize the absence of interagency cooperation at both the federal and state level.

We find that when you say Gimbel's doesn't tell Macy's, as well as Macy's not telling Gimbel's—the same thing is true with the Post Office Department and the EEOC. They'll rehash the same facts and we'll tell them

---

115. *Applying Equal Employment in Trucking, Proceedings of the 16th Annual National Forum on Trucking Industrial Relations* (Washington: American Trucking Associations, Inc.), p. 182.

116. *Ibid.*

117. *Ibid.*

"go to the other department" and they'll say, "Well, we'll do this, we'll get in touch with them." But as a matter of fact, this doesn't happen. We'll square away with the Post Office Department and on the identical facts the EEOC will come in and rehash the thing, and they'll find a charge. They'll go through the entire thing, and if they just manage to find just a little something wrong with you, they'll review your entire company situations.[118]

Needless to say, the companies found these duplications time consuming, burdensome, and expensive. The first time one company learned that a complaint had been lodged against it was when it was disclosed by the *Wall Street Journal.*[119] The company complained to the government because it had not been notified of the discrimination charge. Nevertheless, the company ultimately was visited by the Ohio Civil Rights Commission, the EEOC, the Post Office Department, the National Labor Relations Board, and the local chapter of the National Association for the Advancement of Colored People. Investigations by numerous agencies because of a single complaint prompted a representative from the Southwestern Area Motor Carriers Labor Relations Association to offer the rather caustic observation that, "The number of people that will staff the bureaucracy grows in the inverse order of the problem,"[120] and that he could "envision the day when the staffs of the numerous agencies would be larger than the unemployed." [121] Anticipating that management's problem in dealing with many agencies would not subside, one trucker recommended that the other companies follow his example: write to congressmen from the states where they have terminal facilities.[122]

In an effort to prevent several government agencies from investigating the same complaint, the Post Office Department proposed to the EEOC that the OFCC should be given priority over the complaint cases, but the EEOC would not agree with this. Insisting that it exercise its statutory authority to the fullest, the EEOC intended to handle all complaints submitted to it. In 1966, the EEOC and OFCC adopted a joint poster directing the allegedly discriminated party to write either to EEOC or OFCC.

---

118. *Ibid.*

119. The article, "Bias in the Cab," in the March 31, 1966 issue of the *Wall Street Journal* disclosed the name of this particular company.

120. *Ibid.,* p. 208.

121. *Ibid.*

122. *Ibid.,* p. 211.

In practice, many complainants submitted their case to both agencies. After one agency had conducted a complaint investigation and found no violation, it was not unusual for the other one to question the employer about the same complaint. Rather than inducing companies to assume nondiscriminatory practices, this procedure merely irritated them, as it has in other industries.

There is, of course, another side of the issue—that is, the relative opposition to civil rights in the industry. Only one firm, Bekins Van and Storage Company, joined Plans for Progress in the early stages of the affirmative action doctrine.[123] Few other trucking companies have been leading protagonists of the Civil rights Act or other such measures.

THE ROLE OF THE AMERICAN TRUCKING ASSOCIATIONS

It took less than a year from the promulgation of Executive Order 11246 for the Post Office Department to conclude that the larger trucking firms were not receptive to the objectives of the order. The Department then turned to the American Trucking Associations (ATA) to see if a voluntary trade association could assume a position of leadership regarding equal employment.

The American Trucking Associations, founded in 1933 prior to passage of the Motor Carrier Act, today is a national federation of fifty independent state trucking associations and twelve autonomous conferences representing the various types of carriers. As it endeavors to coordinate the activities of these sixty-two distinct bodies, the ATA's Washington staff also provides member companies with information and data about such topics as the current status of the industry's labor relations problems, federal highway regulations, and operating statistics of the various carriers. The ATA, moreover, is one of the most powerful and sophisticated lobbying agents on Capitol Hill. Individual firms that are close to their respective state trucking associations "can do anything, at any time they may desire, with respect to headquarters and staff." [124]

---

123. For the Bekins story, see Stephen Habbe, *Company Experience with Negro Employment*, Studies in Personnel Policy, Vol. 1, No. 201 (New York: National Industrial Conference Board, 1966), pp. 82-86.

124. *National Organization of the Trucking Industry in the United States*, revised ed. (Washington: American Trucking Associations, Inc.).

Among the twelve conferences are those established to satisfy the needs of certain types of carriers, such as automobile movers, private carriers, regulated carriers, and household movers. Each of these conferences maintains its own staff in Washington, representing the specialized interests of their different kinds of carrier members. A greater degree of power is vested in the state associations, the progenitors of the ATA itself. A trucking company belongs to the ATA only after joining one of the affiliated state associations, which can include all types and classes of carriers. The state associations usually do not engage in collective bargaining at the local level. Their primary function is to represent motor carriers before their state governments, chiefly on regulatory matters.

Prior to the realization in 1964 of "Hoffa's dream"—the signing of the first National Master Freight Agreement (covering mostly carriers of general commodities)—the industry was represented at collective bargaining sessions by distinct areawide employer bargaining units. Hoffa's drive to broaden the geographical scope of the contract forced the industry to establish a comparable national bargaining team. Eventually more than thirty regional labor relations associations were amalgamated into one national bargaining unit, Trucking Employees, Inc. (TEI). TEI has the authority to bargain on all issues, but defers the bargaining of regional conditions to the regional units. This gives rise to the numerous supplementary agreements now appended to the National Master Freight Agreement. Separate but similar multi-employer labor agreements are bargained by labor relations associations or groups covering carriers of special commodities, such as liquid bulk, auto-haul, etc.

If a motor carrier is not affiliated with a regional or state labor association, the IBT sends the company two copies of the newly negotiated agreement, requesting it to sign and expeditiously return one copy. A few companies refuse to join these state associations in the belief that their operating conditions require separate or special terms when they settle with the Teamsters.

The state or regional groups also deal with the union on a day-by-day basis. Believing that they always may be fleeced by the Teamsters, these groups are extremely cognizant of the cost of arousing the IBT's ire. While the ATA may be more sympathetic to the Department's nondiscriminatory goals, as an agency which does not bargain, it can only urge the firms in the industry to take positive steps regarding equal employment opportunities. This function is necessarily limited to working out complaints brought under the grievance procedure of the labor agreement.

Powerless to represent the industry at the bargaining table, the ATA's Industrial Relations Committee provides member firms with information and data relative to all aspects of trucking labor relations. The Committee sponsors an annual forum on such matters as how to handle grievances, motivating middle management, profit-sharing and incentives for trucking employees, and personnel practices in the trucking industry.

The Industrial Relations Committee's 1966 forum was devoted exclusively to the full spectrum of the significance of EEO in the industry. Representatives from the OFCC, EEOC, the Post Office Department, and Department of Justice have addressed these annual meetings. A spokesman for the ATA claims that these annual meetings have provided company representatives with the opportunity to understand the government's most current goals and have served a needed educational function.

CHAPTER VII

Concluding Remarks

It now seems apparent that genuine equal employment of Negroes in the trucking industry is far from a reality. Are there any indications that the future holds promise for the entry of Negroes into the better paying jobs of the industry?

There is some indication, based on a few carefully selected interviews, suggesting that since early 1969 some of the larger carriers have quietly hired or upgraded an increasing number of Negroes. The Teamsters' Union, moreover, has begun to cooperate with the federal government and the IBT now has given its support to a driver training program. The results to date are reputed to have been effective.[125] It is therefore possible that future government, union, and industry cooperation in the area of training may assist Negroes to a greater degree than manpower programs have in the past.

No doubt the several individual complaints of alleged discrimination filed under Title VII of the Civil Rights Act of 1964 and the two pending "pattern of discrimination" suits filed by the U.S. Department of Justice have had some impact upon the industry's former intransigency. Recent studies of the paper and tobacco industries in this series indicate that such litigation can be very effective in situations where union-management attitudes and relationships are antagonistic to the requirements of the Civil Rights Act of 1964.[126] The importance of this judicial prodding is epitomized by one authority who commented, appropos of the Civil Rights Act:

It seems strange, but those who come to evaluate Title VII ten years hence are more likely to find the answers in the files (or lack of them)

---

125. Fred H. Schmidt, "A Repair Shop for Unemployables," *Industrial Relations*, Vol. VIII (May 1969), pp. 280-285.

126. Michael I. Sovern, *Legal Restraints on Racial Discrimination in Employment* (New York: The Twentieth Century Fund, 1966), p. 102.

of the Justice Department than in those of the Commission of Equal
Employment Opportunity.[127]

What was stated about Title VII of the Act is no doubt true
of the contract compliance program. The degree to which the
government enforces (or can enforce) the most recent Executive
Order is likely to determine the trucking industry's employment
of Negroes in the future.

We must concede that there is no reason to believe that the
industry is so adverse to providing equal employment opportunities that it desires to engage in permanent conflict with the government. Once the seriousness of the government's purpose is
well established, we can expect to witness an increased willingness on the part of the industry, and the Teamsters as well, to
take a positive and cooperative position in regard to the hiring
and the training of Negroes and other minorities. Hopefully, it
will not be necessary to resort to that less-than-perfect vehicle,
the rule of law, to resolve the extremely volatile and emotional
problem of equal employment in this industry.

Although the legal posture of the Civil Rights Act of 1964 is
more certain than the legality and latitude of Executive Order
11246, it has been the latter as implemented by the Office of
Federal Contract Compliance and the Post Office Department that
has been of greater significance in promoting equal employment
in the trucking industry. In fact, the Post Office Department
"stands out among federal agencies for its compliance efforts." [128]
Indeed, there are some serious legal problems associated with the
very concept of affirmative action, but many employers, fearing
the worst, have begun to accept equal employment as a necessary
corporate responsibility. Even in the absence of legal bench-
marks, truckers have come to the realization that should the government be compelled to test the latitude of Executive Order
11246, their industry might well be the one chosen for such a
showdown. Because there are so many firms in the industry and
because most of the better-paying jobs require a minimal amount

---

127. See Herbert R. Northrup, *The Negro in the Paper Industry*, Report No.
8 (Philadelphia: Industrial Research Unit, Wharton School of Finance
and Commerce, University of Pennsylvania, 1969); and Herbert R.
Northrup, *The Negro in the Tobacco Industry*, Report No. 13 (Philadelphia: Industrial Research Unit, Wharton School of Finance and
Commerce, University of Pennsylvania, 1970).

128. United States Commission on Civil Rights, *Jobs and Civil Rights*, prepared by the Brookings Institute, Clearing House Publication No. 16
(Washington, D.C.: U.S. Government Printing Office, 1969), p. 143.

of training, a debarment procedure against a single firm would not reduce significantly the transportation services provided by public motor carriers.

This study began by noting that in 1967 some Negro youths in Cincinnati blocked the passage of white drivers when they noticed that there were relatively few Negroes possessing these coveted jobs. The forming of this barricade by these Negro youths was a contributing factor to the racial confrontation that subsequently occurred.

In his classical exposition of *An American Dilemma*,[129] Gunnar Myrdal maintained that there was a disparity between the dictates of what he referred to as the American Creed of equality of opportunity and the manner in which whites treated Negroes. He believed that eventually there would be a bridging of the gap between the espoused principles of equality and the actual implementation of these principles. Theoretically, the wedding of ideal and action would take place when a tortured white conscience could no longer live with this inherent contradiction between ideal and action. Events have demonstrated that the Negro will wait no longer to see whether the white community will change its attitude toward him. What the youth in Cincinnati did demonstrates a singular incident in which Negroes have taken power into their own hands and have therefore made clear that they are capable and willing to accelerate the rate of social change and adaptation.

If power, therefore, be the vehicle by which the Negro is to gain the full exercise of his rights, including equal employment opportunities, then hopefully power channeled through existing governmental institutions is, in the long run, capable of aiding the Negro in his quest for equality. From the known to the unknown is a valid inference—we can infer that only with continued governmental efforts will the Negro find the trucking industry's doors always and everywhere open to him.

---

129. Gunnar Myrdal, *An American Dilemma* (New York: Harper & Row, 1944); also Arnold Rose, *The Negro in America* (New York: Harper and Row, 1948), p. 312. The second work offers a succinct comment on Myrdal's major thesis.

Appendix A

SAMPLE SELECTION

The 3,397 individual firms comprising the total population of this study must annually report to the Interstate Commerce Commission the number of people on their payrolls. The most recent published source from which these employment data could be obtained was *Trinc's Blue Book of the Trucking Industry* (1966 edition), and not the ICC Reports. These employment data were taken from this former publication. These employment data, in conjunction with 1960 census data were the bases upon which a representative sample of the 3,397 firms was selected. A detailed explanation of the criteria employed in the aggregation process, and of the statistical methods used in the selection of the sample firms is presented below.

1. Using a specially designed card, pertinent information about each of the 3,397 companies was systematically catalogued. Included on these cards was such information as: the name of the carrier, the type of carrier, total number of hourly employees, and the location of the firm's corporate headquarters.

2. The forty-six Standard Metropolitan Statistical Areas, with the largest total population according to the 1960 Census, were listed in an array. The choice of these forty-six SMSA's was predicated upon the fact that the 1960 Census reported nonwhite male truckdrivers and deliverymen for these areas only. It initially was assumed that these nonwhite data were relevant in the research, but this assumption proved to be wrong. Numerous trucking companies are headquartered in Winston-Salem and Greensboro, North Carolina. Therefore, the population criterion was relaxed, as was the availability of data relevant to nonwhite truckdrivers and deliverymen, and the SMSA's located in North Carolina were included in this study. Although the 1960 Census lists the Winston-Salem and Greensboro SMSA's independently, they were treated as one SMSA in the study. As a result, the geographical area, or the labor markets comprising the total population of the study consisted of forty-eight selected SMSA's. According to the 1960 Census, these forty-eight contain 42.3 percent of the nation's total population, and 9,559,240 or 46.6 percent of the nonwhite population.

3. Companies were separated according to the SMSA's in which their corporate headquarters fell. Consequently, 1,548, or 45.6 percent, of the 3,397 Class I and II carriers claimed one of the forty-eight SMSA's as the area in which their corporate headquarters were located. In 1965, these 1,548 firms employed 46.3 percent or 274,115 of the hourly personnel on the payrolls of all Class I and II carriers. The remaining 1,349 or 54.4 percent of the carriers which employed 305,502 or 53.7 percent of the hourly employees were not considered in the study.

4. The country was then divided into four geographical regions. Several factors were considered in determining the geographical scope of these four regions. First, an effort was made to include in each specific area those states possessing somewhat homogeneous attitudes regarding the racial problem. Second, the cost associated with having to interview firms in noncontiguous areas was seriously weighed. Third, these areas were determined so as to obtain a reasonable distribution of the employees in each of the four areas. Tables A-1 through A-4 show the particular SMSA's found in each of the areas, and the number of employees accounted for by both large and small firms having their corporate headquarters in these same SMSA's.

5. Once the total number of employees for each SMSA was determined, the SMSA's were listed in a descending order according to the total number of employees reported by firms with corporate headquarters in the respective SMSA's. For example, in the Northeast area the SMSA's were listed in the following order: New York, Philadelphia, Boston, Pittsburgh, Newark, Baltimore, etc. Then, these employment statistics were cumulated, and a random sample of SMSA's was selected in such a way that the probability of an SMSA being included in the sample was proportional to the industry's total hourly employment. Sample SMSA's for each region were randomly chosen so that the selected sample areas included approximately 50 percent of the industry's total number of hourly workers employed by the firms having their corporate headquarters located in each of the broad geographical areas. The sample SMSA's are shown in Table A-5.

6. After the sample SMSA's, thirteen in number, were chosen in a random manner, it was necessary to select sample firms with headquarters located in each of the SMSA's. To prevent selecting a disproportionate number of large firms, the companies in each SMSA were clustered into two distinct groups. All com-

TABLE A-1. *Trucking Industry*
Total Hourly Employees by Size of Firm
10 SMSA's, Northeast Region, 1966

SMSA	Total Firms	Total Hourly Employees	Number of Large Firms	Hourly Employees Large Firms	Number of Small Firms	Hourly Employees Small Firms
New York	113	23,406	20	19,062	93	4,344
Philadelphia	93	12,862	19	10,377	74	2,485
Boston	66	7,078	16	5,243	50	1,835
Pittsburgh	57	6,564	13	5,357	44	1,207
Newark	33	3,203	7	1,023	26	2,180
Baltimore	23	3,126	8	2,582	15	544
Jersey City	42	2,439	4	1,427	38	1,012
Buffalo	21	1,700	4	1,138	17	562
Washington	15	895	2	405	13	490
Rochester	6	321	—	—	6	321
Total	469	61,594	93	46,614	376	14,980

Source: *Trinc's Blue Book of the Trucking Industry,* 1966 Edition (Washington: Trinc Associates, Ltd., 1966).

TABLE A-2. Trucking Industry
Total Hourly Employees by Size of Firm
15 SMSA's, South Region, 1966

SMSA	Total Firms	Total Hourly Employees	Number of Large Firms	Hourly Employees Large Firms	Number of Small Firms	Hourly Employees Small Firms
Winston-Salem Greensboro	13	11,198	7	10,943	6	255
Dallas	22	7,917	9	7,470	13	447
Charlotte	18	5,805	8	5,217	10	588
Atlanta	20	4,738	5	4,142	15	596
Houston	23	4,288	7	3,671	16	617
Birmingham	19	3,078	8	2,600	11	478
Memphis	17	2,909	3	2,352	14	557
Tampa	8	2,056	4	1,845	4	211
San Antonio	7	1,633	4	1,558	3	75
El Paso	5	1,442	4	1,400	1	42
Miami	8	1,055	2	878	6	177
Louisville	13	790	3	314	10	476
Fort Worth	7	743	2	518	5	225
Norfolk	11	627	1	428	10	199
New Orleans	8	486	1	384	7	102
Total	199	48,765	68	43,720	131	5,045

Source: Trinc's Blue Book of the Trucking Industry, 1966 Edition (Washington: Trinc Associates, Ltd. 1966).

TABLE A-3. *Trucking Industry*
Total Hourly Employees by Size of Firm
12 SMSA's, Midwest Region, 1966

SMSA	Total Firms	Total Hourly Employees	Number of Large Firms	Hourly Employees Large Firms	Number of Small Firms	Hourly Employees Small Firms
Chicago	146	27,976	39	23,560	107	4,416
Detroit	52	13,597	27	12,866	25	731
Akron	22	11,672	11	11,307	11	365
St. Louis	57	7,904	22	6,721	35	1,183
Cleveland	43	8,331	19	7,332	24	999
Minneapolis-St. Paul	38	6,975	18	6,168	20	807
Columbus	18	6,781	9	6,457	9	324
Milwaukee	33	4,084	11	2,983	22	1,101
Cincinnati	22	3,590	11	3,115	11	475
Indianapolis	20	3,479	5	2,636	15	843
Toledo	11	1,082	3	688	8	394
Dayton	8	377	—	—	8	377
Total	470	95,848	175	83,833	295	12,015

Source: *Trinc's Blue Book of the Trucking Industry*, 1966 Edition (Washington: Trinc Associates, Ltd., 1966).

TABLE A-4. Trucking Industry
Total Hourly Employees by Size of Firm
11 SMSA's, West Region, 1966

SMSA	Total Firms	Total Hourly Employees	Number of Large Firms	Hourly Employees Large Firms	Number of Small Firms	Hourly Employees Small Firms
San Francisco	61	21,703	14	20,031	47	1,672
Los Angeles	134	15,736	29	12,105	105	3,631
Denver	36	9,690	12	8,840	24	850
Kansas City	32	8,535	12	7,847	20	688
Seattle	34	3,590	8	2,483	26	1,107
Oklahoma	15	3,410	5	3,010	10	400
Portland	34	1,905	8	988	26	917
Tulsa	14	1,309	3	795	11	514
Phoenix	15	1,027	2	514	13	513
Omaha	13	798	2	402	11	396
San Diego	6	205	—	—	6	205
Total	394	67,908	95	57,015	299	10,893

Source: Trinc's Blue Book of the Trucking Industry, 1966 Edition (Washington: Trinc Associates, Ltd., 1966).

TABLE A-5. *Trucking Industry
Sample SMSA's by Region*

Region	Sample SMSA's	TotalNumber of Hourly Employees	Percent of All Employees in Region
Northeast	1. Philadelphia	12,862	20.88
	2. Boston	7,078	11.49
	3. New York	23,406	38.00
	Total	43,346	70.37
South	1. Winston-Salem Greensboro	11,198	22.90
	2. Charlotte	5,805	11.91
	3. Birmingham	3,078	6.31
	4. Atlanta	4,738	9.71
	Total	24,819	50.83
Midwest	1. Chicago	27,976	29.10
	2. St. Louis	7,904	8.24
	3. Detroit	13,597	14.18
	Total	49,477	51.52
West	1. San Francisco	21,703	31.96
	2. Denver	9,690	14.27
	3. Los Angeles	15,736	23.17
	Total	47,129	69.40

Source: Data in author's possession.

Note: The SMSA's are arranged in the order they were randomly
selected. Because Philadelphia and Boston accounted for only 32.4
percent of the total number of employees in the Northeast area,
it was necessary to select another SMSA. In so doing, New York
was chosen and therefore the total number of employees in the
three samples exceeds the 50 percent criterion initially established. A similar situation arose in the West.

panies reporting 100 or less workers employed throughout their operations were in one group, while firms with 101 or more employees were included in the second group. Using employment data as the criterion, the firms in each group were listed in a descending array, and then these employment statistics were cumulated. After the firms were collated into two distinct clusters, and the firms employment statistics cumulated, a random sample of firms was selected in such a way that 20 percent of all firms having 101 or more employees were chosen, and 10 percent ers, and the firms, employment statistics cumulated, a random The 10 and 20 percent limits established for small and large firms respectively were not rigorously adhered to in those cases where the total number of firms in each cluster was less than ten. The total number of large and small firms found in the selected SMAS's, as well as the number of firms chosen in the sample, are shown in Table A-6. Mention is made in the text of those instances where the firms initially selected refused to cooperate in this study, and when, therefore, resampling was necessary.

TABLE A-6. *Trucking Industry*
Total and Sample Firms by Firm Size
Selected SMSA's

SMSA	Total Number of Large Firms	Number of Large Firms in Sample	Total Number of Small Firms	Number of Small Firms in Sample
Philadelphia	19	4	74	7
Boston	16	3	50	5
New York	20	4	93	9
Winston-Salem Greensboro	7	2	6	2
Charlotte	8	2	10	2
Birmingham	8	2	11	1
Atlanta	5	2	15	2
Chicago	39	8	107	10
St. Louis	22	4	35	4
Detroit	27	5	25	3
San Francisco	14	3	47	5
Denver	12	3	105	3
Los Angeles	29	6	24	10
Total	226	48	602	63

Source: Data in author's possession.

Appendix B

EXPANSION OF THE EMPLOYMENT DATA AND DETERMINATION OF THE COEFFICIENT OF VARIATION FOR FOUR GEOGRAPHICAL AREAS

Four statistical procedures were used to adjust the original employment data and determine the coefficient of variation. The first three of these procedures expanded the data in such a manner that Negro-white employment data are presented on the bases of four distinct geographical areas. First, the racial employment statistics are reported on the bases of thirteen SMSA's. It was then possible to expand the SMSA data so that they represented the racial employment profile for four distinct geographical areas. (See Appendix A for details.) Third, the data were aggregated to reflect the percentage of Negroes employed by the trucking industry in forty-eight SMSA's. The exposition below uses either small or large firms in its examples, but it was necessary to follow the identical procedure for both large and small firms in all instances.

1. Adjusting the data for the thirteen selected SMSA's

The sample small firms in each SMSA were selected in proportion (10 percent) to the number of small firms in each SMSA, and the original data were expanded according to:

$$\frac{\text{Total Number of Firms in the SMSA}}{\text{Total Number of Selected Sample Firms in the SMSA}}$$

This ratio then was multiplied by the original data obtained for each job classification. After doing this for all the job classifications and for large and small firms, the adjusted statistics for large and small firms were summarized. This statistical method of adjustment was used in compiling the employment data for each of the sample SMSA's.

2. Adjusting the data for four distinct broad geographical areas

The sample SMSA's for each of the four broad regions were randomly chosen so that the selected SMSA's included approximately 50 percent of the industry's total number of workers in each of the four geographical areas. The original employment data were expanded according to the ratio below:

$$\frac{\text{Total Employees for All the Small Firms in the Region}}{\text{Total Employees for All Small Firms in Each Sample SMSA}}$$

The ratio was multiplied by the number of employees in each job classification, as derived by the method explained above. This methodology was employed in adjusting the data for each of the sample SMSA's in the four broad regions. To obtain the regional totals, the further expanded data were summarized. For example, the number of Negro and white local drivers employed by small firms in Boston, New York, and Philadelphia were aggregated, making it possible to ascertain the percentage of Negro local drivers in the Northeast.

3. Procedure used to determine the Negro-white employment profile for forty-eight SMSA's combined

The aggregating of the employment data for forty-eight SMSA's was facilitated because statistical adjustments were made at the SMSA and broader geographical levels. The four combined regions contained a total of forty-eight SMSA's and an employment profile reflective of race was attained by adding the number of employees in each of the four regions. This was done on the bases of large and small firms, according to specific job classifications, and total statistics were obtained by adding the large and small firm adjusted employment data.

4. The determination of the coefficient of variation

After expanded employment data were determined, the estimated number of Negroes and the coefficient of variation associated with it was then computed. The coefficient of variation was computed for the four broad geographical areas only, and for the expanded adjusted statistics of both the large and small firms. These results are presented with the appropriate tables in the text proper.

Appendix C

POST OFFICE DEPARTMENT GUIDELINES ON AFFIRMATIVE ACTION UNDER EXECUTIVE ORDER 11246

"Affirmative Action" as defined in Section 202 (1) of Executive Order 11246 is a relatively new concept in contract management. The attached material has been prepared to acquaint Government contractors with this requirement.

Definition

Affirmative action means positive, firm or aggressive action as opposed to negative, uncertain or passive action. Affirmative action encompasses the steps necessary to insure that a contractor puts into practice his stated policies of equal employment opportunity without regard to race, color, creed or national origin.

Application

Employment (hiring); upgrading; demotion or transfer; recruitment or recruitment advertising; layoff or termination; rates of pay or other forms of compensation; and selection for training (on the job), including apprenticeship.

Examples

1. Publication and dissemination of written policy of equal employment opportunity.

2. Appointment of equal employment policy officer charged with responsibility of securing compliance and advising corporate officials of progress.

3. Establishment of system of control and feedback to assure application of policy at all levels.

4. Orientation lectures for all supervisory personnel as well as employees to insure familiarity with policy.

5. Inclusion of policy statement in all employee-management publications (newsletters, magazines, etc.).

6. Notification in writing to all recruitment sources that the contractor, as an Equal Opportunity Employer, *solicits* referral of qualified applicants without regard to race, color, creed, or national origin.

7. Secure statement in writing from employee bargaining representatives (unions) indicating that their policies and practices are consistent with the provisions of the Orders.

8. Post SF-38 (Notice to Unions) in conspicuous areas of plant.

9. Modify existing collective bargaining agreements, where necessary, to include nondiscriminatory clause and eliminate restrictive barriers established by:

   a. Dual lines of seniority based on race;

   b. Dual rates of pay based on race; and

   c. Dual lines of promotion or progression based on race.

10. Discontinue use of employee referral system as sole source of recruitment unless proven to be administered so as to assure reasonable racial mix of applicants.

11. Broaden recruitment sources to include referrals of qualified minority group applicants.

12. Insure that employment prerequisites are administered equitably. (Education and/or testing factors should not create disadvantage for minorities.)

13. Re-evaluate qualifications of lower echelon minority group employees to insure equal consideration for job progression based on standards and qualifications which should be no higher or no lower than those established for white employees.

14. Solicit directly the support of responsible and appropriate community agencies to assist in recruiting efforts.

15. Solicit cooperation of academic and vocational schools to establish curricula which will provide the skills and education necessary to fulfill manpower requirements.

16. Consider establishing new training program and classes in facilities where outside programs are inadequate or unavailable to minority groups.

17. Invite minority groups to tour facilities and receive explanation of Equal Employment Opportunity program.

18. Seek, employ and develop minority group personnel, as well as others, in white collar classifications.

19. Eliminate segregated washrooms, cafeterias, smoking areas, locker rooms, drinking fountains, time clocks, pay lines, contractor-sponsored recreational programs, etc.

20. Display EEO posters in conspicuous areas throughout the plant.

21. Use of approved slogan, emblem or statement in all recruitment advertising media.

22. Remove all reference to race, color, creed or national origin from *pre-employment* applications.

23. Maintain racial identity in post-employment files separate and apart from active personnel folders or records.

Index

Affirmative action, 101-107
  Post Office definition, 101-102
Alliance for Labor Action, 65-66
American Trucking Associations, 2n,
    3n, 8n, 11n, 22n, 61n, 110n,
    127-129
  Industrial Relations Committee, 97,
    129
  and training programs, 110
Ashby, William T., 9n
Associated Transport, Inc., 121
Automobile Manufacturers Associa-
    tion, 10n

B and P Motor Express, 124
Beck, David, 30-31
Bekins Van and Storage Company,
    127
Bradshaw v. Associated Transport,
    Inc., 121, 121n
Braswell Motor, 119-120
Bush Hog, Inc., 66n

Center for Research in Marketing,
    Inc., 16n
Central Motor Lines, Inc., 123-124
Civil Rights Act of 1964, 66, 97-98,
    106, 113, 114n, 120, 124, 130-
    131
  compliance agencies, 124-127
Commercial Car Journal, 48n, 99n
Consolidated Freightways, 13
Court cases, 114, 124, 130

Delehanty, George, 7n
Dobbs, Farrell, 21, 82
Doriot, Georges F., 46n
Driver qualifications, 19, 40-42, 49-
    50, 88, 98

Employment
  occupational distribution
    blue collar, 20
    white collar, 19, 23
  racial-occupational segregation, 28-
    29
  work force, 18, 22-24
Employment and Earnings, 5n
Equal Employment Opportunity Com-
    mission, 1, 5, 33, 97-98, 124-
    127

Executive Orders, 94, 94n, 95, 95n, 98,
    101, 102, 112, 113n, 131
Featherson, Clarence H., 106, 107n
Fitsimmons, Frank, 65
For-hire carriers, 1-3, 10-18
Fortune, 13

Garnel, Donald, 30n
Georgia Highway Express, 114-117
Gibbons, Harold, 65
Greyhound Lines, 104
Grievance procedures, 49, 55-56, 100

Habbe, Stephen, 127n
Hairston v. McLean Trucking Com-
    pany, 118, 118n, 119
Harris, Abram L., 21n
Hoffa, James, 21, 29-30, 82n, 128
  and Negro rights, 30, 64
  and Post Office recommendations,
    96-98

Industry structure, 2-3, 5, 8-18, 22
  concentration, 13-16
  family ownership, 8
  government regulation, 9-10, 53,
    104, 109
  location, 16-19
International Association of Machin-
    ists, 60n
International Brotherhood of Team-
    sters, Chauffeurs, Ware-
    housemen and Helpers of
    America, 2, 2n, 5, 9, 20-22,
    60n
  and American Trucking Associa-
    tions, 128
  Councils, 66n
  ethnic bloc control, 73, 83
  locals, 21, 29-31, 99
  membership, 20-21, 29-30
    anti-Negro sentiment, 21-22, 88,
    99
    Negro membership, 20-21, 31
  and Negro employment, 29-32, 48-
    53, 56
  Negro organizers in, 31
  Proceedings, 65n
  racial policies of, 22, 29-32, 64-67,
    98-101, 130-131
    civil rights contributions, 65-66

constitution, 31, 31n
court cases against, 123-124
influence in hiring, 50-53, 74-76,
    82, 88
Southern Conference, 82
International Teamster, 20n, 40n, 66n
Interstate Commerce Act of 1940, 9
Commission, 3, 9-10, 16n

James v. *Braswell Motors*, 119-120
James, Estelle Dinerstein, 21n, 30n,
    56n
James, Ralph C., 21n, 30n, 56n
Richard Johnson, Jr., v. *Georgia
    Highway Express*, 114-117

Kiley, Edward V., 22n

Labor demands, 22-24
Landrum-Griffin Act of 1959, 30
Lansing, John B., 10n
Lee v. *Observer Transportation*, 117-
    118
Legal Defense and Education Fund,
    124
Leiter, Robert D., 28, 28n
Leone, Richard D., 5n

McFarland, Ross A., 42n
McLean Trucking Company, 118-119

Manpower, 18-24
Methodology, 3-7
Modern Automotive Services, Inc.,
    118-119
Moseley, Alfred L., 42n
Motor Carrier Act of 1935, 9-10, 40,
    127
Motor Freight Supplemental Agree-
    ment, 59n
Motor Freight Transportation and
    Warehousing (SIC 42), 5
Myrdal, Gunnar, 75n, 132, 132n

Nagle, Paul A., 95-101, 102n
National Advisory Commission on
    Civil Disorders *Report*, 1n
National Forum on Trucking Indus-
    trial Relations, 61n, 103n,
    104n, 125n, 126n
National Labor Relations Act, 67
    Board, 66-67
National Master Freight Agreement,
    50, 50n, 53n, 96, 128
and seniority, 53-54

Supplemental Agreements, 53, 54n
Negro employment
    1920-1940, 8-9
    1940-1960, 25-32
    1960's, 33-67, 107-109
    and industry location, 16-18, 57-58
    influence of Teamsters, 45-50
    job performance, 43-45, 104
    occupational distribution, 25, 33-40
        blue collar, 35, 107
        white collar, 35, 73, 107
    percentage of jobs, 1, 33, 35, 38, 68
    by regions, 9 25, 28, 38, 68-93
    and strikebreaking, 21
    in warehouses, 25
"Negro jobs," 8-9, 21, 75
Negro truck drivers, 1, 35, 38, 58, 82,
    98, 105, 107
    lack of seniority, 53
    in Post Office Department, 42-46
    and qualifications, 40-42
    Teamster attitude toward, 65, 82,
        97
New York State Commission Against
    Discrimination, 46n
North Carolina Driving School, 121
Northrup, Herbert R., 23n, 29n, 131n

Observer Transportation, 117-118
Occupational distribution
    clerical, 63-64
    dispatchers, 63
    local drivers and helpers, 58-60
    management, 61-63
    nondriver workers, 60-61
Office of Federal Contract Compli-
    ance, 98-101
    and affirmative action, 102-103, 124-
        127
    and debarment of companies, 101,
        113, 124
Over-the-road drivers
    Teamster organization of, 21
    wages, 42

Patton, D. K., 7n
President's Committee on Equal Em-
    ployment Opportunity, 97-98
Private carriers, 2, 10
Public carriers
    see For-hire carriers

Quarles v. *Philip Morris, Inc.*, 106n

Race Relations Law Review, 66n

Racial employment policy of companies, 13, 42-43, 45-46, 49, 98-101, 66-67
  discriminatory practices, 114-124
    departmental segregation, 118-119
    and driving partners, 99-100
    in hiring, 20, 45-46, 48-53, 99, 105, 118, 120, 122
    in promotions, 116-118, 120, 123
    in wages, 117
  economic consequences, 47
  governmental pressure, 49-93-129
  of Post ffice Department, 42-46, 98-101
  Post Office study and recommendations, 96-98, 105
  and segregation in public accommodations, 28, 57
  of Teamsters, 45-50, 64-67, 98-101
  and white employees, 47-48, 98
Racial-occupational segregation, 28-29, 95-96
Risher, Howard W., Jr., 29n
Roadway Express, 122
Romer, Sam, 30n
Rose, Arnold, 75n, 132n

Schmidt, Fred H., 130n
Segregation
  public accommodations, 28, 57
  company facilities, 100
Seniority, 41, 53-55, 93
  departmental, 118-119
  influence on Negro, 53, 55, 93
  and job bidding, 42, 54
  and partner choice, 42, 54, 100
Southwestern Area Motor Carriers Labor Relations Association, 126
Sovern, Michael I., 130n
Spero, Sterling D., 21n
Sylvester, Edward C., 102-103

Teams Drivers International, 20
Teamsters
  see International Brotherhood of Teamsters
Technological changes, 75-76

Tobin, Daniel, 21, 29-31
Training programs, 20, 41, 48, 105
  as affirmative action, 110-113
  government pressure for, 112
Trinc's Blue Book of the Trucking Industry, 3n
Trucking Employees, Inc., 128

Unionization, 20-22
United Automobile, Aerospace and Agricultural Workers, 65
United Federation of Postal Clerks, 125
United Parcel Service, 51
United States
  Bureau of the Budget, 11n
  Bureau of the Census, 5
  Bureau of Labor Statistics, 23n
  Commission on Civil Rights, 131n
  Department of Justice, 66, 106, 113, 121-123
  Department of Transportation, 9, 40, 40n, 41-42
  Post Office Department, 45n
    complaints and hearings, 100-101, 113
    compliance reviews, 94-98, 106-107, 124-127
    and industry efforts, 98-101
    Negro drivers in, 42-46, 104
    and Teamsters, 96-98
United States v. *Associated Transport*, 121, 121n
United States v. *Central Motor Lines, Inc., et al.*, 123-124
United States v. *Local 189, United Papermakers and Paperworkers, et al.*, 106n, 123n
United States v. *Roadway Express*, 122, 122n

Wages
  drivers, 42
  nondriver workers, 61-62, 64
  Post ffice Department, 45
  in South, 76
Wall Street Journal, 22n, 23n, 99n, 126n
Wiley, Bell Irvin, 75n